7867

595.7
DIC

The World of Butterflies

The world of
BUTTERFLIES

Text by
Michael Dickens

Photographs by
Eric Storey

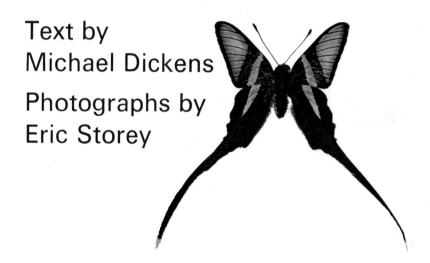

Osprey

We wish to dedicate this book to Arthur Macdonell Morley, the Kent lepidopterist.

Published in 1972 by
Osprey Publishing Limited, 707 Oxford Road, Reading, Berkshire
© Copyright 1972 Michael C. Dickens and Eric S. Storey
All rights reserved
SBN 85045 086 1

Printed by
The Berkshire Printing Co. Ltd., Reading

Preface

Both the author and photographer of this book are deeply concerned for the future of butterflies and moths on this planet. By showing you, the reader, the wonderful and inimitable colour and pattern of these frail creatures of indescribable beauty, we hope to impress upon you the importance of their preservation.

Of all the creatures on earth, the life pattern of butterflies and moths is amongst the most difficult to comprehend. Their metamorphosis, from egg through caterpillar to pupae and finally adult, is a scientific wonder. They do help to pollinate blossom, provide food for birds and control the growth of weeds, but beyond this they play only a minor part in the balance of nature. It would almost seem that butterflies and moths are on this earth for man's enjoyment alone, for their pure beauty, as one of the very few 'free' pleasures remaining to us. Every effort should be made to conserve them.

It is by understanding butterflies and moths, in particular their life-history, that we come to realize their true importance to man. This knowledge may, if acted upon fast enough, save the many hundreds of species already in danger of extinction. In some countries the collection and sale of certain species is already prohibited by law; but this is not enough, as it only *defers* their eventual doom.

The finest butterfly and moth fauna comes from the tropical regions of the world, and here, at this very moment, man is at work opening up the jungles for his financial gain, with little thought for the indigenous creatures who live there. What will become of the butterflies? They will be extinct—the result of man's ultimate crime against nature. In all civilized countries, development is unavoidable; more land is constantly needed for housing and cultivation, but always at the expense of the natural countryside that is so often considered wasteland. It is this land which we must conserve, for it is here that wildlife of all types is to be found, and butterflies are amongst those most quickly affected by any change in environment. We must act now to conserve large areas of land, stop the use of certain pesticides, and breed and release species in danger of extinction. But this can only be achieved with the thought in mind that the most important gains to man are not always financial ones. The work of protecting and increasing rarer species will be expensive, but we hope that somewhere in the world there are benefactors who would wish to involve themselves with either money or labour towards the aims we have in mind.

We envisage butterfly and moths farms in each climatic zone of the world, where work can be carried out with the co-operation of scientists and enthusiasts to release the live species in carefully-selected areas of each zone. These areas of land will have to be protected from 'progress', but as we are now beginning to help the plight of wildlife, let us hope that the insect world will not be forgotten.

You may wonder how one can sell butterflies and yet at the same time wish to conserve them. A butterfly farm can breed in captivity with 100 per cent success; in the wild only about 10 per cent survive to maturity. Thus, if greater numbers are released than were originally caught, and the correct conditions prevail, the wild population must be increased. Then, as purchase of specimens is the best way to create an interest in butterflies, the surplus can safely be sold. It is often the schoolboy breeding from caterpillars who grows up to understand fully the life-history of the butterfly, and subsequently realizes the importance of conservation. Indeed, it is just such a train of events which has influenced the author's life.

There is no better place from which to acquire stock than a reputable dealer; the alternative is to catch or find your own specimens. This is fine if the species is common, but amateurs have been known to exterminate by over-collection, and the collector is easily tempted to take more than he needs. The field is better for observation than collection: watch butterflies, paint them, photograph them, *but do not remove them* unless you are able to return more than you take.

This book is not intended purely as a scientific work. Its technical detail is certainly accurate, but it is primarily a means to fire in all of you that same enthusiasm for nature as in ourselves, and the desire to protect our world of butterflies.

Michael C. Dickens

Eric S. Storey

Acknowledgements

Many people have contributed to the preparation of this book and we would like to thank them for their help.

All the photographs are of actual specimens we have purchased or borrowed over the last few years since this book was originally conceived. We have endeavoured to obtain the most up-to-date information available on all the species illustrated.

In particular we wish to thank the following for their kind co-operation:

Mr. Arthur M. Morley, for the use of his library.
Mr. John H. Drake, for permission to photograph his specimens.
Mr. S. K. Sircar, of India.
Mr. R. Nardin, of Guyana.
Mrs. R. H. Morgan, of New Zealand.
Mrs. L. Martinez, of Peru.
Mr. M. Hummelgen, of Brazil.
Mrs. P. McNear, of South Africa.
Mr. J. Kesselring, of Brazil.
Mr. S. K. Ong, of Taiwan.
Mr. L. Godart, of Central African Republic.
Mr. J. J. Raj, of India.
Mr. A. Low, of Great Britain.
Mr. E. Palik, of Poland.
Mr. J. Weiss, of Brazil.
Mrs. R. Heng, of Malaya.

Contents

---

70 *Ornithoptera priamus urvillianus*
71 *Ornithoptera priamus poseidon*
72 *Ornithoptera priamus croesus*
73 *Schoenbergia paradisea*
74, 75 *Schoenbergia goliath*
76 *Papilio antimachus*
77 *Papilio zalmoxis*
78 *Papilio zagreus*
79 *Papilio sesostris*
80 *Papilio neophilus*
81 *Papilio nireus*
82 *Papilio demoleus*
83 *Papilio thyastes*
84 *Papilio protesilaus*
85 *Papilio weiskei*
86 *Papilio philoxenus*
87 *Papilio hector*
88 *Papilio menestheus*

89 *Papilio arcturus*
90 *Papilio paris*
91 *Papilio crino*
92 *Papilio machaon*
93 *Papilio thoas*
94 *Papilio ulysses*
95, 96 *Teinopalpus imperialis*
97 *Armandia lidderdalei*
98 *Leptocircus meges*
PIERIDAE
99 *Eurema brigitta*
100 *Prioneris thestylis*
101 *Delias hyparete*
102 *Delias descombesi*
103 *Catopsilia philea*
104 *Ixias pyrene*
105 *Appias nero*
106 *Hebomoia glaucippe*
107 *Colotis regina*
108 *Colotis danae*

Introduction

HISTORY

The first known work on natural history to be published in Britain was Sir Theodore de Mayerne's *Theatorum Insectorum* in 1643. This was written originally in Latin but was later translated into English. In this work there appeared a section on butterflies of all countries. It is probable that the practice of collecting butterflies goes back much further than this, for modern interest in zoology stems from the times when the explorers of the fifteenth century began to discover many new lands, and returned with curios of what they had seen. In the latter part of the seventeenth century the first serious collections were made in England. The first book on British butterflies only was published in 1717, entitled *Papilionum Britanniae*, written by James Petiver; at this time he knew of forty-eight species. The first work in colour was published in 1720: *The Natural History of English Insects* by Eleazar Elgin.

In those ancient days people concerned with entomology were titled Aurelians, perhaps after the golden chrysalids of some butterflies (perhaps the Small Tortoiseshell). It was in 1735 that Carl von Linne (better known as Linnaeus) published his work *Systema Naturae,* which introduced the system of giving two names to identify a species (binomial nomenclature), as is still used today. This is discussed later in the section on Classification. It was Linnaeus who first called butterflies 'Lepidoptera', from the Greek meaning 'scale-wing'.

Providing butterfly specimens are properly looked after they will last a very long time. The author of this book has some butterflies dating from 1750 that are still in excellent condition and hardly faded at all.

It is interesting to note how the number of known species of butterflies has increased over the years as more and more have been identified. In 1758 Linnaeus identified 192 species; by 1775 Fabricus had listed 406; in 1823 Latreille and Godart named 1,802; and by 1871 Kirby was able to list 7,695. We cannot give the present number as no one has had the patience to count them, but the figure is in excess of 50,000 different species of butterfly. And new species are still being discovered every year.

CLASSIFICATION OF BUTTERFLIES

In a book of this size it is neither wise nor possible to attempt to describe in detail such a complicated system as the classification of butterflies. There are already many scientific works available which do this very adequately. It suffices to explain that many taxonomists differ in opinion as to the correct number of the *families* of butterflies. Briefly the primary system of classification runs as follows:

Order: Lepidoptera (i.e. all butterflies and moths).

Sub-order: Heteroneura (this includes many moths and most butterflies: those having hind wings smaller than fore wings; also having different neuration, or vein patterns, on the fore and hind wings).

Superfamily: Papilionoidea (the butterflies proper).

The super-family is divided up into the various families of butterflies, as listed below. This system for classifying butterflies may seem rather confusing to the amateur, but is used here so that the classification is given which we consider is correct, in case it is required.

The following are the now-accepted families of butterflies, together with a few of the best-known common vernacular names given in parentheses. It should be noted that these common names are of no value to a serious collector as they are not, of course, universally used, whereas a scientific name can be instantly understood by anyone in any country.

Families of the Heteroneura (butterflies)

SATYRIDAE	(Browns, Satyrs, etc.)
DANAIDAE	(Monarchs, Tigers, Lacewings, Crows, etc.)
ACRAEIDAE	(Acraeas)
HELICONIIDAE	(Heliconiids)
NYMPHALIDAE	(a vast group including Vanessas, Fritillaries, Nymphs, etc.)
BRASSOLIDAE	(Owls, etc.)
MORPHIDAE	(Morphos)
AMATHUSIIDAE	(Palms, Owls not the same as above, etc.)
LIBYTHEIDAE	(Snouts or beaks, etc.)
RIODINIDAE	(this family includes the ERYCINIDAE, which are considered by some as a separate family)
LYCAENIDAE	(Blues, Coppers, Hairstreaks, etc.)
PAPILIONIDAE	(Swallowtails, Kites, Birdwings, Mines, Apollos, etc.)
PIERIDAE	(Whites, Yellows, Sulphurs, Jezebels, Tips, etc.)
HESPERIIDAE	(Skippers, etc.)

The *family* may be divided into *subfamilies,* and these in turn may be divided into *tribes.* Following these comes the *generic* name or the name given to a closely-related group of species all of which will have this name. Within the genus comes the second or *specific* name to identify a particular species within the genus. It may be further necessary to divide species into *subspecies* and this additional name is used where a species can be divided into groups distinguishable from one another by characteristics; they will also come from different areas. The words *type species,* or as it is known in the US, *nominate subspecies,* refer to the original race to which the specific name was first given and this will have the specific name repeated as the sub-specific name. Finally as part of the name one may include the initials in an abbreviated version of the author responsible for its description. Thus in the case of a butterfly named and described by Linnaeus we find *Nymphalis antiopa L.*

REGIONS OF THE WORLD

When considering different types of butterfly, the world may be divided into several parts. The fauna of the world is so immense that it is convenient to use these geographical divisions. These divisions are partly geographical and partly climatic. In this book we will make reference to the following regions:

PALAEARCTICA: covering Europe, Asia and North Africa, from the Arctic to the tropics. This is a temperate region.

AFRICANA: all Africa south of the Sahara Desert (including Madagascar and part of Arabia).

INDO-AUSTRALICA: India south of the Himalayas, southern China, Malaysia, all islands from Japan to New Zealand, New Guinea, Australia, etc. This is a tropical region except to the south, which is temperate.

NEARCTICA: Arctic Canada and America as far south as Mexico. This is a temperate region.

NEOTROPICA: tropical Mexico, Central and South America, and all the islands in the area. This is the second tropical region.

Sometimes the two Americas are placed together under the division *Americana.* Sometimes *Palaearctica* and *Nearctica* are combined to give the *Holarctic* region; the only problem with this is the almost impossible size of the region thus formed.

LIFE HISTORY OF BUTTERFLIES

For those who are complete beginners to the subject we will here discuss briefly the various stages in the life-cycle of a butterfly.

Ovum The word ovum means 'egg', and the plural is ova. Selecting only a suitable type of plant, the female butterfly will deposit there her egg, which she then sticks to the plant. Almost every species of egg is different, and the species of the butterfly can often be accurately identified from examining its eggs alone. The female may lay all her eggs at once in a lump, or she may lay only one on each leaf, or often only one egg on each tree; some even drop their eggs on the ground. The number eventually laid may be anything from about twenty up to two hundred. Providing the egg is not going to spend the winter in this state, it will hatch into the larva (caterpillar) in between three and fourteen days (hatching fastest in tropical climates).

Larva The sole purpose, one may think, of the larva or caterpillar is to eat. This certainly appears to be true, for the larva will eat so fast that it has to discard its non-elastic skin four or five times during its life. Some larvae only eat at night; others may try to avoid being eaten by being covered in long or even poisonous hairs. Unless it is hibernating, the larva will achieve full growth in anything from two to eight weeks; then it sheds its final skin to reveal the chrysalid.

Chrysalis This is a special term for the butterfly pupa; it is enclosed in a silken cocoon. The chrysalid is apparently always a dormant stage, and in temperate climates often a hibernating stage. But it is in this stage that the whole cell structure will break down and re-form itself so as eventually to become the butterfly. Chrysalids always hang suspended from something attached by a pad of silk produced by the larva. This may leave it hanging upside-down, or upright with an additional girdle of silk around the middle for support. After a period of one to four weeks (or up to six months in hibernation) the inner transformation will have taken place, and the butterfly is ready to emerge.

Imago The adult butterfly, or imago, emerges from the split shell of the chrysalis and climbs up the stalk (or whatever else the chrysalis was attached to), and prepares to expand its wings. On first emerging, the insect is complete except that its wings are only a fraction of their eventual size. It is first necessary to pump them up, which the butterfly does by forcing fluid into them from its body. After about half an hour the wings are fully developed. A further half hour or so is needed before the wings are completely dry. Then the butterfly is ready to fly and to prepare for a whole new cycle.

Adult butterflies live for about two or three weeks, but less, of course, if they meet any enemies in that period. But the species which hibernates as adults during the winter in temperate climates can live for up to a year.

The male will recognize his mate by the scent she produces and by colour perception. To attract the females, the males have scent scales on their wings, or glandular scales or hairs on their bodies, wings or legs. Some of the species in this book (for example, *Agrias sardanapulus* on page 32) have these hairs clearly visible. But such scent glands take many forms and are highly complex; they are often not easy to detect. Many of the very pleasant scents are easy for the human nose to pick up.

PARASITES AND ENEMIES

At all stages of their life-cycle butterflies are in danger of attack from birds, spiders, beetles and many other creatures that prey on them. Larvae and chrysalids are frequently attacked by flies and wasps. Many more fall victim to parasites. In almost all cases the host will eventually die once the parasites have bred within its body.

In tropical areas lack of food-plants in periods of drought is also a significant cause of death.

But man himself is the worst enemy of all, cutting down the forest, ploughing, planting, irrigating, draining, and over-collecting (for sale) rare species. In fact any alteration of the habitat of a species greatly endangers its survival.

PROTECTION

Without going into too much detail on this very complex subject, it is enough to say that many butterflies in all stages of their development have had to adapt in order to survive. In the first place the ova are usually laid underneath a leaf, and often match the colouring of their surroundings. Larvae likewise may also be leaf-coloured, or they may be hairy; some do not look like larvae at all but resemble other, more fearsome creatures.

But it is the adult imago which has perhaps developed the most individual methods of protection. If you look at the Leaf Butterfly *(Kallima inachus)*, its camouflage method is instantly apparent. Many species have an underside which will blend in with their surroundings. Others, like the Morpho butterflies, rely on a flash of bright colour as they fly off to deter their would-be attackers. Some species imitate the colouring of other types which are distasteful to enemies, especially birds (some even resemble bees or wasps). Some look like twigs or leaves. Others simply drop to the ground and feign death if they are touched. Often, to protect their bodies from attack they have prominent eye-spots on their wings: aiming for this a bird may peck out a piece of the wing which will leave the butterfly to escape without any ill effect.

STRUCTURE AND SENSES

Butterflies have no internal skeletal structure; instead all the delicate organs are enclosed within a framework of chitin.

Proboscis All adult butterflies have a *proboscis,* or tongue, even if only a very rudimentary one, and this is generally kept coiled up underneath the head. They feed on nectar, and sometimes on rotten fruit or decaying matter. Many also drink water and tree-sap. They locate their food by sight and scent.

Respiration Butterflies do not breathe in by means of lungs, but by allowing air to diffuse into a system of very fine tubes, which eventually taper off to become very minute and so allow the air to pass directly into the cells. This process is the same for larvae. Expiration involves a similar procedure, but diffusion to the outside is through the outer body surface. It is this particular method of breathing which necessarily limits the size of butterflies.

Sight Butterflies have very good sight for the detection of movement, but it is not good for clear images of objects at a distance. There is no doubt that they have some colour vision.

Blood In a butterfly the blood is free-flowing inside most of the body cavity, and is generally not confined within tubes or arteries. This makes the creature particularly vulnerable to any kind of injury, which can easily prove fatal. There is a primitive heart extending along the body, which keeps the blood in circulation.

Digestion operates in much the usual way. Food enters through the proboscis into the storage sac. There digestive juices are secreted, and the products of digestion are absorbed through the walls of the gut. The waste products are excreted through the end of the gut.

Genital organs These differ in virtually every species of butterfly. So it is possible to identify the species by dissection and examination of the genitalia alone.

Sense organs These are well developed in the butterfly. They are found in the setae, or small hairs, on various parts of the body, on the wings, and on the legs. With these it can actually taste, and it can thus identify both food-plant suitable for laying eggs on and food for the butterfly itself to feed on. It can smell through its antennae (males of some moth species can detect a female—who often emits a scent—over considerable distances). It is also through the antennae that a butterfly is able to achieve balance and find direction in flight. Some authorities believe that butterflies can also hear: over most of the body they have organs with drum-like structures which vibrate like the human eardrum.

Colours in butterflies are produced either by pigment on the scales, or by diffraction of light, or by surface structure. In the latter two cases the processes are complicated, but it is the actual structure of the scales that produces colours such as the iridescent blue of the Morphos. The colours of butterflies are very important for their camouflage.

REARING IN CAPTIVITY

Anyone can catch and kill a butterfly, but how many have actually bred them? It is not difficult to obtain perfect specimens and keep them in captivity. Naturally in temperate climates one has to have the food-plants available and be able to provide sunlight as well as controlled temperature and humidity. This is bound to be time consuming and could also be costly. Fortunately some exotic butterflies adapt well to improvised conditions.

To explain techniques of rearing in detail would require an entire book on its own, so we can but summarize the requirements in brief. Having obtained some stock, usually chrysalids, these should be allowed to emerge; damp is needed with heat. The adults, when flying, should be given a large flight area in a sunny place so that they will mate (this can be done by hand). The food-plants should be put into the same breeding house (sometimes small cages will suffice) as the fertile female will only produce ova as long as she is properly fed. If the ova hatch whilst still attached to the food-plants and the larvae are kept from wandering away, the next stage is easy. Additional potted plants can be introduced so that the larvae crawl across to them. Finally they will pupate on the same food-plants or on the new foliage. If conditions remain suitable the imago will soon emerge and the whole cycle may begin anew.

Correct conditions, food-plants and luck all help. Disease can occur and then everything may be lost, but if one can reproduce natural conditions there is a fair chance of success.

For those already living in the tropics half the work is already done. It is to be hoped that they will breed large numbers in captivity for release later on, for losses in nature are very high (probably seventy-five per cent never reach maturity), but in captivity the losses should be as low as ten per cent. In this way man can help to restore some of what he is taking away.

EXPLANATION OF TEXT NOTES

The following notes should be carefully studied, since they explain how to use the information which accompanies each photograph. The illustrations are grouped by families (the fourteen families of butterflies are listed on page 12 in the Introduction). Not all families are represented in this book. Generally the families can be further divided into sub-families, but we have not felt this necessary for the purpose of this book.

Purpose

The purpose of the notes under each illustration is to give concisely all the basic information about the species, without excessive use of technical terms. It is specifically intended that these notes should be clearly and easily understood by all.

Sex

Under each photograph is a symbol indicating the sex of the specimen illustrated. Males are shown by the symbol ♂ and females by ♀. The reason for thus indicating the sex of the specimen will become clear when you read the note on sexual dimorphism below.

Scientific name and family name

All specimens in natural history are given a scientific name. This name will be made up of several parts (see under Classification, page 12). First is the generic name (the name of the genus)—for example, in the first illustration this is *Hestia*. This is followed by the specific name (the name of the species)—in our example this is *leuconoe*. This is followed by the sub-specific name (which identifies this particular race of the species)—in our example it is *clara*. It is important to give the name of the overall family in which the whole genus is included—in this case it is Danaidae. Thus the correct name for the first illustration, on page 23, is stated: *Hestia leuconoe clara*, of the family Danaidae. This scientific name is used universally, by all natural historians everywhere. Note that in some cases, for clarity, we have added the sub-specific name (e.g. *clara*) under the heading 'Scientific Name', but normally this will be found below, in italics under the heading 'Sub-Species and Similar Species'. Sometimes the sub-specific name is not quoted.

Wingspan

It is important to note that wingspan cannot be measured merely by placing a ruler across the fore wings and measuring the distance from wing-tip to wing-tip. The correct wingspan is found by doubling the measurement from the tip of the fore wing to the centre line of the thorax at the point where the wings meet the thorax. This measurement does not vary however the wings are set, and it gives a span that is never much different from that of the the creature when it was still alive. For the purposes of the book this span is measured in centimetres; some species vary greatly in size (or even between the two sexes). Where appropriate, the approximate size variation is indicated; an average specimen would have a span midway between these two extremes.

Range

Records of range for exotic butterflies are bound to be inaccurate. Collectors, fortunately, are not everywhere; records are not always kept; many areas are quite inaccessible; and many species tend to wander. All that is possible is to plot all points on a map where a certain species has been observed and verified, and to join together all the points. From this can be deduced the places where the species is most common. By discounting the instances where it was obviously an odd migrant, and by relating such to the type of vegetation, it is possible to remove all areas where the species would not occur. The result will be a rough estimation of the range of the species.

The areas covered by many species are often so enormous that it would take a lifetime to define the actual distribution of even a single species. The impossible has not been attempted in this book and we have indicated only the overall range for each species. The specimen may vary in frequency throughout its range or be equally common everywhere; it may only occur in a few places within the range; it will only prefer certain areas of vegetation—thus, in fact, unless huge in scale an accurate map could not even be attempted. We have therefore decided to encircle the entire known range within which the species may be found, only leaving out places where the species is not normally found. For the sake of clarity the lines are drawn outside the range perimeter.

Habits and habitat

It is a pity that so many collectors do not bother either to try to breed what they catch, or to keep a record of all the circumstances, vegetation and surroundings. Nor do they note down the habits of the insect they seek. This means that little is known about the majority of exotic butterflies. For the purpose of this book we have worked closely with collectors all over the world, but it will be many years before the gaps are even partly filled in.

When reading the notes it should be remembered that the same species may behave differently and be found in various types of habitat as one moves within its range. The notes can only be a generalization.

Food-plants

Often the larvae of a particular family will eat the same food or related foods throughout its range. Listed are those foods that are known to be eaten by the species in question. Sometimes only the family is named, sometimes the actual species. In many cases the food-plant is either unknown or has never been identified; maybe one day this information will become available.

Sexual dimorphism

As with most living things there is often a considerable difference between the male and the female. With butterflies there are often details of shape, pattern or colour which vary between the sexes, and this information is briefly given where it is not illustrated. But sometimes the sex can be determined only by dissection of the abdomen; which is usually larger in the female.

Sub-species

Many species vary in colouring, shape or pattern, depending on the location or habitat type. Where it is considered relevant, these are listed in the notes. Likewise mention is made where a species alters from season to season (seasonal dimorphism), or where a species has several different forms (polymorphic). This information is limited to describing only certain forms and sub-species, usually the ones that are best known.

Similar species

Species within the same genus, and those of other families but of similar appearance are noted. Here again the information is restricted to the better-known species. It is outside the scope of this book to include complete lists.

1

♂

Scientific name	*Hestia leuconoe*
Family	Danaidae
Common name	Giant Wood Nymph
Wingspan	13·5–15·5 cm.
Range	Taiwan, Philippines, Palawan, Malaysia, Borneo, Sumatra.
Habits and habitat	Floats along like a piece of paper being blown in the wind, a weak flier, usually never leaving the forest. Often follows the course of a small stream or floats high up in the flowering trees. Often pairs will settle in the trees in the later afternoon. In Taiwan flies March to August.
Food-plants	The life-history is not known.
Sexual dimorphism	Sexes very similar; females generally larger.
Subspecies and similar species	The form illustrated is *H. leuconoe clara* from Taiwan (Formosa). There are many other named races throughout the region. This is an extremely variable species. Similar are many species such as *H. hypermnestra* and *H. idea.* There is also the group of similar but much smaller Idea species.

2

♂

Scientific name	*Euploea diocletianus*
Family	Danaidae
Common name	Magpie Crow
Wingspan	8–9 cm.
Range	Sikkim, Assam, Burma, Laos, Vietnam, Thailand, Malaysia, Borneo, Sumatra, Java, Celebes.
Habits and habitat	Found at all elevations but generally only up to the foothills. Males are found along forest roads, at wet patches, banks of streams, coming into the open. The females keep to the trees, flying higher than the males. When alive they have a most unpleasant smell.
Food-plants	Asclepias species and other plants.
Sexual dimorphism	The female is almost lacking the blue lustre, and the ground colour is brownish. Males have a sex gland on the hind wings.
Subspecies and similar species	The illustration shows *E. diocletianus diocletianus* (previously rhadamanthus) from the Malay Peninsula area. There are a vast number of other Euploea species but none with the Magpie markings.

3

♂

Scientific name	*Danaus plexippus*
Family	Danaidae
Common name	Monarch/Milkweed/Wanderer
Wingspan	9·5–10·5 cm.
Range:	Throughout North America (migrates to Canada), Australia, New Zealand (introduced into these countries); also New Guinea and other islands in that area.
Habits and habitat	Although found in North Canada, it does not breed there. Can fly great distances, often sailing along with the wings held open. Flies over seas at great height but can settle and rise again easily. This butterfly has a strong, unpleasant odour when alive. In the U.S.A. the winter quarters are in Florida, west to Mexico and California, in semi-hibernation, often massed in trees. Fond of flowers. In some areas continuously brooded; in others hibernates as adult and more rarely as chrysalid. Very distasteful to birds and very tenacious of life.
Food-plants	Asclepias species (milkweeds), Apocynum, Acerates, Calotropis, Aranjia.
Sexual dimorphism	The male has the scent organ clearly visible on the hind wings. This the female lacks; also is paler and veins darker.
Subspecies and similar species	There are several named forms, and very similar is *D. archippus,* This species used to be given the same name but has white spots on the fore wings. Also similar are *D. chrysippus* (Africa, Asia, Indo-Australia) and *D. genutia.* In Central and South America is the dark race, *D. plexippus megalippe.*

4

♀

Scientific name	*Heliconius doris delila*
Family	Heliconidae
Common name	Red Doris
Wingspan	8–9 cm.
Range	Guianas, Brazil, Bolivia, Peru, Ecuador, Colombia.
Habits and habitat	As for H. doris (see page 27) a species of dry open scrubland and bush. Flies all year round in hottest weather.
Food-plants	Passiflora (passion-flower) species.
Sexual dimorphism	Sexes almost identical.
Subspecies and similar species	*H. doris* is an amazing butterfly, not only being extremely variable but in that it exists in three colour forms: blue (see page 27) red (as above) and green (rare). There are many similar species, often difficult to identify.

5

♀

Scientific name	*Heliconius doris*
Family	Heliconidae
Common name	Doris
Wingspan	8–9 cm.
Range	Found throughout all of South America north of Argentina.
Habits and habitat	Flies all year round, even in the dry period when little else is to be seen. Scrubland and bush country, in the open. Settles often, flies near the ground. Often many specimens fly together; never shy; they sometimes drink at river banks.
Food-plants	Passiflora serrato digitata and other Passiflora species.
Sexual dimorphism	Male and female very similar.
Subspecies and similar species	The illustration is of the type form, there being many variations and two other main colour forms of this one species. Besides blue it may be red (see page 26) or even the rare green colour. In fact *H. doris* is probably the most variable of all the Heliconidae.

6

♀

Scientific name	*Heliconius phyllis*
Family	Heliconidae
Common name	None
Wingspan	7–8 cm.
Range	North Argentina, Paraguay, south Brazil, Bolivia, Peru.
Habits and habitat	Commonly found along coastal roads or at openings into the forest, clearings within woods, and frequently in gardens. Settles on flowers and shrubs, often many at a time and generally together with other species. This species has an unpleasant odour when alive. Flies all year round but least common in the new year.
Food-plants	The life-history is unknown but no doubt it feeds on a species of Passiflora.
Sexual dimorphism	Both sexes very similar; the female is larger.
Subspecies and similar species	This species is mimicked by another, *Nymphalid E. lansdorfi.* There are several rather similar species but few have the very bright colours: for example *H. petiverana, H. favorinus, H. amaryllis.*

7

♂

Scientific name	*Hypolimnas dexithea*
Family	Nymphalidae
Common name	None
Wingspan	11–12 cm.
Range	Madagascar (Malagasy Republic) only found in the northern and eastern parts of the island.
Habits and habitat	Strictly a forest species, little known of its habits.
Food-plants	Life-history unknown.
Sexual dimorphism	Sexes almost identical.
Subspecies and similar species	This species is unlike all the other *Hypolimnas* species.

8

9

8♂   9♀

Scientific name	*Hypolimnas bolina*
Family	Nymphalidae
Common name	Great Eggfly
Wingspan	8·5–10·0 cm.
Range	A large range from Ceylon and India east through South China to Taiwan, south through the whole of Malaysia and Indonesia, including the Philippines, to New Guinea and Australia.
Habits and habitat	Found in open places, this is a lowland species rarely ascending very high. May be seen in plantations, gardens, or on the edges of forests. Some years there are great numbers and the following year they may be very sparse. A female often stays on one flower all her life. Males are very pugnacious, keeping every day to the same spot when not chasing off intruders. In some areas males congregate on tree trunks, they also may roost in numbers. Continuously brooded in some areas.
Food-plants	Elatostama cuneatum, Fleurya interrupta, Sida retusa, Sida rhombifolia, Asystasia scadens, Ateruantherea denticulata, Portulaca oleracea, Pseuderanthemum variable, etc.
Sexual dimorphism	Sexes dissimilar, as illustrated. Females are extremely variable.
Subspecies and similar species	This species is extremely variable. Especially in the polymorphic females, of which there are hardly ever two examples alike. The illustration shows the race *H. bolina nerina* from Australia (and the adjacent isles) this form being very similar to that from Java. There are a vast number of *Hypolimnas* species, some difficult to identify, the best-known and most common is *H. missipus* (Africa, India, etc.). Seasonal variation is also prominently shown in the above species.

31

10

11

10 upper side ♂   11 under side ♂

Scientific name	*Agrias sardanapulus lugens*
Family	Nymphalidae
Common name	None
Wingspan	9–10 cm.
Range	Upper Amazon, Peru and Bolivia.
Habits and habitat	Seen in sunny clearings of forests, especially in hot weather between the seasons. Impossible to catch in flight, this species comes to tree-sap or mud along the road, when it can be taken, although still very wary. Flies all year round. Males rest at one particular spot from where they fly off and return to exactly the same spot which may be a leaf high up in a tree. Flying on very hot days from midday, always singly, at lower elevations. They never leave the forest and often circle round tree tops.
Food-plants	The life-history is quite unknown.
Sexual dimorphism	The female is not so bright, the hind wing having almost no blue. The wings are more rounded. The fore wing never has blue as well as red.
Subspecies and similar species	Originally *A. sardanapulus* was listed as a form of another species. *A. claudia,* to which it is very similar. There are several named races; some examples have no blue beyond the red area on the fore wings, others have reduced amounts of blue on the hind wings.

33

12

13

12 upper side ♀   13 under side ♀

Scientific name	*Argynnis childreni*
Family	Nymphalidae
Common name	Large Silverstripe
Wingspan	9–10 cm.
Range	Kashmir, Nepal, Sikkim, Assam, Burma, south-east China.
Habits and habitat	Found in Himalayas up to 13,000 feet. Not in woods but prefers the grassy slopes at their edges, or on hill-tops. Often drinking at damp patches in India. Flies May to October. Normally two broods per season.
Food-plants	Probably Violaceae.
Sexual dimorphism	Sexes very similar: females usually larger.
Subspecies and similar species	Similar is *A. pandora,* but neither this nor any other *Argynnis* species has such a bright silver under side.

14

♀

Scientific name	*Prepona antimache*
Family	Nymphalidae
Common name	Silver King Shoemaker
Wingspan	10·5–12·0 cm.
Range	South America, as far south as Paraguay and Uruguay.
Habits and habitat	The live insect has a delicious fragrance of vanilla. Found in forests especially at excrement or rotting fruit. Unless feeding it flies high in trees and remains hidden, only appearing when it is very hot and sunny. Produces a crackling noise in flight. Can be baited, ideally in a forest clearing. Never moves far from breeding grounds and males take up post on one spot chasing away intruders and always returning to this spot. A lowland species is rarely seen in mountains. On wing in early morning, sometimes flying even when it is dull.
Food-plants	Anonaceae and Abacata trees.
Sexual dimorphism	Sexes almost identical; females usually larger.
Subspecies and similar species	There are a considerable number of different *Prepona* species, many being very similar on the upper side, and even though the under sides are a means of identification generally even these vary considerably. The *Prepona* species are very similar to the Charaxes group. Similar is *P. demophon.*

15

♂

Scientific name	*Cethosia biblis*
Family	Nymphalidae
Common name	Red Lacewing
Wingspan	8–9 cm.
Range	Nepal, Sikkim, Bhutan, Assam, Burma, south-east China, Malaysia, Borneo, Sumatra, Java, Celebes, Moluccas, Philippines.
Habits and habitat	Found within forests and along forest borders and at river edges, often on flowers. Generally only found in lowland hills but does occur in Sikkim up to 7,000 feet. Flies all year round except in India (March to December only).
Food-plants	Passiflora.
Sexual dimorphism	The usual female form is greenish instead of red, but there are several forms, the most extreme being virtually the same colour as the male. Note, the under side is 'lacewing' patterned in all shades of red and orange.
Subspecies and similar species	This is an extremely varied species showing seasonal variation. There are many named forms; our illustration is of *C. biblis timena,* the typical Indian form. There are a number of similar species such as *C. cyane, C. nietneri* and *C. hypsea,* etc.

16

17

16 ♂   17 ♂

Scientific name	*Cyrestis thyodamas*
Family	Nymphalidae
Common name	Common Map
Wingspan	6–7 cm.
Range	Kashmir, Nepal, Sikkim, Bhutan, Assam, India, Burma, south-east China, Taiwan, Japan.
Habits and habitat	Found in hilly jungles up to 8,000 feet. Drinks at damp patches, sometimes in number. Feeds at flowers; often seen near streams. Hides under leaves. In flight like a piece of paper suddenly seized by the wind. Females stay in deep forest. Flies all year round, except in the Himalayas (March to December).
Food-plants	Ficus indica, Ficus nemoralis, Ficus glomerata, Ficus religiosa, Ficus bengalensis (banyan).
Sexual dimorphism	Males and females almost identical.
Subspecies and similar species	We illustrate both the form *C. thyodamas thyodamas* (16), the typical Indian form, and *C. thyodamas formosanus* (17), the race from Taiwan; these show a typical example of differing geographical races. Considerable seasonal variation is evident in this species. The wet season form is more heavily marked and has a white ground colour; the dry season form is usually yellowish in ground colour. Similar are several species such as *C. nivea, C. cocles*.

18

Scientific name	*Kallima inachus*
Family	Nymphalidae
Common name	Orange Oakleaf/Indian Leaf
Wingspan	10–12 cm.
Range	Kashmir, Nepal, Sikkim, Assam, India, Burma, south-east China, Taiwan.
Habits and habitat	Generally found in the undergrowth in woods, or on river banks, drinking. Rarely rises above tree-tops. Particularly fond of rotting fruit, especially bananas, and can be baited. Despite its wonderful camouflage, if disturbed it flies away to settle with wings still open. Found in Sikkim up to 8,000 feet. A species of the valleys, normally it remains hidden with the wings closed, exhibiting the finest camouflage of any butterfly in the world. Two broods per season in India.
Food-plants	Giradinia heterophylla, Polygonum orientalis, Strobilanthus capitatus.
Sexual dimorphism	Sexes almost identical: the female is usually larger, the fore wing tip less hooked.
Subspecies and similar species	Shows distinct seasonal variation in the Indian region. Elsewhere there are many named forms. The illustration shows the race from Taiwan; this unbelievably is surpassed by the Indian race which shows even more variation. Similar is *K. paralekta* (Malaysia).

19

♂

Scientific name	*Cymothoe sangaris*
Family	Nymphalidae
Common name	Blood Red Cymothoe
Wingspan	6–7 cm.
Range	Sierra Leone, Guinea, Ivory Coast, Ghana, Nigeria, Cameroons, Central African Republic, Gabon, Congo, Angola, Uganda, Kenya.
Habits and habitat	Confined to the forest areas. Flies all year round. Nothing else known.
Food-plants	Life-history not known.
Sexual dimorphism	The female has a grey upper side with orange brown at the base of the wings; it is variable.
Subspecies and similar species	Similar are *C. coccinata* and *C. aramis* both not so bright red. There are other species or perhaps only subspecies.

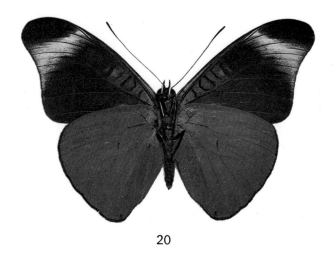

20

♀

Scientific name	*Panacea prola*
Family	Nymphalidae
Common name	None
Wingspan	6–8 cm.
Range	Venezuela, Colombia, upper Amazon, Ecuador, Peru.
Habits and habitat	Generally a mountain species often found resting on tree trunks, especially those bordering roads.
Food-plants	Probably Dalechampia species.
Sexual dimorphism	Sexes identical. Illustrated is the under side. The upper side has a band of greenish-yellow; the hind wing band is more blue and the ground colour is a steel-blue sheen.
Subspecies and similar species	Similar are *P. chalcothea* (Colombia) and *P. regina* (Peru).

21

♀

Scientific name	*Vanessa atalanta*
Family	Nymphalidae
Common name	Red Admiral
Wingspan	6·5–7·5 cm.
Range	North Africa, all Europe to 62° North, Asia Minor, to Iran; Canada, North America and south to Guatemala, the Antilles; and New Zealand (introduced). May be found further north but probably migrating examples.
Habits and habitat	Flowery banks, gardens, rough ground up to 6,000 feet. Migrates, coming to England in the spring. Found as far north as the Arctic Circle. Partial hibernation of adults in winter months. In Europe flies from May to October. Loves flowers, fruit, and tree-sap. Normally two broods per season.
Food-plants	Urtica (nettles), also Humulus (hops), Parietaria (pellitory), and other Urticaceae. The larvae are solitary feeders.
Sexual dimorphism	Sexes are very similar; the female is perhaps larger.
Subspecies and similar species	Similar is *V. indica* (from India, China, Canaries, etc.). *V. gonerilla* is the most exciting relative (from New Zealand). In Africa proper there are two species very similar but with tails, of the genus Antanartia.

22

♂

Scientific name	*Salamis temora*
Family	Nymphalidae
Common name	Blue Salamis
Wingspan	8–9 cm.
Range	Nigeria, Cameroons, Central African Republic, Congo, Sudan, Uganda, Kenya, Ethiopia, Gabon, Angola, Zambia, Tanzania.
Habits and habitat	A species of the forest, both lowland and lower mountain. Flies all year round. Often settles on trees.
Food-plants	Life-history unknown.
Sexual dimorphism	The female is larger than the male: The blue area is more restricted, the borders wider and greyish-pink.
Subspecies and similar species	Similar is *S. cytora*, but the blue is lighter and less intense.

23

♂

Scientific name	*Metamorpha dido*
Family	Nymphalidae
Common name	Bamboo Page
Wingspan	9–10 cm.
Range	From southern North America through all of Central America and South America as far as Paraguay and Uruguay.
Habits and habitat	Flies singly, often over a particular area time and time again. Rests on vines and sometimes feeds on flowers. Found in open places, scrubland and in gardens. Does not drink at water. Often circles high over trees in hottest sun.
Food-plants	Passiflorae such as P. laurifolia and others.
Sexual dimorphism	Sexes almost identical: The female is larger with more rounded wings. (The under side is similar but is shaded in silvery-green, and brown markings replace the black of the upper side.)
Subspecies and similar species	*M. dido wernickei* as illustrated, is the common subspecies, with rich green and darker black; underneath the bands are more uniform and narrow. The type form occurs only in the northern part of the region. Similar is *V. steneles*.

24

♂

Scientific name	*Precis hierta*
Family	Nymphalidae
Common name	Yellow Pansy
Wingspan	5–6 cm.
Range	Arabia, Sudan, Ethiopia and all Africa south of the Sahara.
Habits and habitat	Bush, savannah, open woodland, and frequently at flowers in garden. Flies all year round.
Food-plants	Barleria, Justicia, Asystasia, Choeloranthus, Ruellia.
Sexual dimorphism	The female is similar to male: the yellow area on the hind wings is enlarged and there is a mark of black in the yellow of the fore wings.
Subspecies and similar species	Probably this species originated in India, where there occurs a very similar species. A subspecies is found in Madagascar (Malagasy Republic).

25

♀

Scientific name	*Precis oenone*
Family	Nymphalidae
Common name	Blue Pansy
Wingspan	5·5–6·5 cm.
Range	All Africa south of the Sahara.
Habits and habitat	Savannah, open woodland, bush country, and often seen in gardens. Fond of flowers. Flies all year round.
Food-plants	Asystasia coromandeliana.
Sexual dimorphism	The female is larger than the male: also the eye-spots are much larger.
Subspecies and similar species	*P. oenone* should be compared with *P. orithya* from the Indo-Malayan area which is very similar and no doubt originated from the same species. A subspecies is found in Madagascar.

26

♂

Scientific name	*Callithea leprieuri*
Family	Nymphalidae
Common name	None
Wingspan	6·5–7·0 cm.
Range	The lower Amazon in Para Province of Brazil; also recorded in Surinam.
Habits and habitat	A species of the jungle found along rivers, attracted to decaying matter or ripe fruit. Often flying high in trees. Little is known about this species.
Food-plants	The larvae have poisonous hairs and live singly, but the creeper on which they feed is not named.
Sexual dimorphism	The female is very similar to the male but not so bright in colour: the blue area is reduced and the greenish marginal band enlarged.
Subspecies and similar species	There are several other species of *Callithea* (easily recognized by their under sides) that have an overall blue sheen. The best known is *C. sapphira*, a superb iridescent violet-blue, also *C. freyja* is often seen, a vivid medium blue. Probably *C. leprieuri* is the commonest of the genus.

27

♀

Scientific name	*Catagramma sorana*
Family	Nymphalidae
Common name	None
Wingspan	5–6 cm.
Range	Brazil, Bolivia, Paraguay.
Habits and habitat	Found in the low-lying jungles. Loves to sit high up on a tree or chase around tree tops. Generally found near a river or stream, only coming down to feed.
Food-plants	The life-history is unknown.
Sexual dimorphism	The female illustrated is a little larger than the male. The male has the markings in bright red and the blue is less obvious, showing only as a deep violet overall sheen, fore wing apex markings are not white but ochreous.
Subspecies and similar species	*Catagramma* species are on the upper side red, blue, yellow or a combination of these colours. *C. sorana* is quite unlike the others in the genus; even its criss-cross patterned under side is unusual.

28

♂

Scientific name	*Catagramma excelsior*
Family	Nymphalidae
Common name	None
Wingspan	6·0–6·5 cm.
Range	Ecuador, Peru and the upper Amazon.
Habits and habitat	Found in the mountain forests; often sits high in the trees when not darting about, rarely settling for long. Feeds at decaying matter.
Food-plants	Probably Allophylus.
Sexual dimorphism	The female lacks the blue iridescence.
Subspecies and similar species	There are several forms of the above species, illustrated is *C. excelsior pastazza* from Ecuador and Peru. One form has red on the fore wings.

29

29 ♂   30 ♂   30

Scientific name	*Callicore neglecta*—(upper side)
	Callicore clymena—(under side)
Family	Nymphalidae
Common name	Figure of Eight/Jewel Butterfly
Wingspan	4·5–5·0 cm.
Range	All Central America and the west of South America as far south as Paraguay.
Habits and habitat	Mountain species very frequently found at flowers or in the forests. Fond of rotting fruit. Fly all year round.
Food-plants	Probably Trema micrantha.
Sexual dimorphism	Sexes almost identical, the female has more prominent markings. Both upper sides are almost identical.
Subspecies and similar species	There are several very similar species and races of the above, making them very difficult to identify. Illustrated is the race of *C. clymena peruviana* from Peru and Bolivia.

♂ 31

Scientific name	*Eunica alcmena*
Family	Nymphalidae
Common name	None
Wingspan	7·0–7·5 cm.
Range	Mexico, all Central America, Venezuela, Colombia, Ecuador, Peru.
Habits and habitat	Flying on sunny days, this species is found in the mountain forest areas, usually keeping to the shade in the trees. Always flies alone, often drinking at wet patches. Likes rotting fruit and can be attracted to lures. Several specimens may gather when feeding. Also rests on tree trunks.
Food-plants	The life-history is unknown.
Sexual dimorphism	The female is brown with a white band across the fore wings and does not have the blue iridescence.
Subspecies and similar species	There are several similar species with varying amounts of blue on the wings, but none has the same degree of brightness. A form of *E. alcmena irma* from Peru has even more blue and is perhaps even more splendid than the race illustrated.

32

♂

Scientific name	Charaxes eupale
Family	Nymphalidae
Common name	Green Charaxes
Wingspan	6 cm.
Range	Sierra Leone, Guinea, Ivory Coast, Ghana, Nigeria, Cameroons, Central African Republic, Congo, Uganda, Kenya, Tanzania, Angola.
Habits and habitat	Found in forest areas, often feeding on tree-sap, rotten fruit, excrement and other decaying matter. Easily baited, never feeding from flowers. The males frequent wet patches. Flies all year round.
Food-plants	Scutia and Albizia.
Sexual dimorphism	The female is very similar to the male, but usually larger.
Subspecies and similar species	Very similar is the species *C. eupale dilutus* (Congo area), often classified as a subspecies.

33

♂

Scientific name	*Nymphalis antiopa*
Family	Nymphalidae
Common name	Camberwell Beauty (in Britain) Mourning Cloak (in U.S.A.)
Wingspan	6–8 cm.
Range	West Europe across temperate Asia to perhaps 70° north (as migrant in extreme north), and south to the Himalayas. Throughout North America and Canada (migrant in north).
Habits and habitat	Found in woods, gardens and open country (especially roadsides) often feeding at sap or resting on tree trunks. Lowlands and hills. Flies singly on sunny days and not easy to catch. Also fond of rotting fruit and can be baited. On the wing from July, and may live for a year. Two or three broods in U.S.A., one in Europe.
Food-plants	Willow, poplar, elm, birch. Larvae are gregarious, usually on a solitary tree that is used every year. Many losses from birds and parasitic flies.
Sexual dimorphism	Sexes almost identical; the female is usually larger.
Subspecies and similar species	There are no similar species. The form in most of Europe has very light, almost plain, creamy borders; the one in U.S.A. has darker borders speckled with grey-brown. Rare varieties have no definable borders and even no blue spots on the wings (variety hygea).

34

♂

Scientific name	*Apatura iris*
Family	Nymphalidae
Common name	Purple Emperor
Wingspan	7·5–8·5 cm.
Range	West Europe, across Asia to 60° north, to Japan. Absent in Scandinavia and much of southern Europe.
Habits and habitat	Found in low-lying old-established woods and around their edges, drinking on damp roads or at puddles. Most of the day they fly high or sit high in trees, from where they make sorties, returning to the same spot. The females rarely descend from the tree tops. They love excrement of all types and can be baited. Fly from June to August all sunny days. Always found singly. Best times to see them are early morning, when both sexes may settle on the ground, and occasionally in the early evening. One brood per season. Larvae hard to find. Very difficult to obtain ova in captivity.
Food-plants	Salix caprea (sallow), and other Salix species, Populus tremulae.
Sexual dimorphism	The female is larger and without the blue sheen; white markings and band are also enlarged.
Subspecies and similar species	In Europe there is the similar but smaller *A. ilia*. There are several named forms of *A. iris. On the wing the female looks like a giant White Admiral (L. camilla). Similar species are few, A. ambica* (India), *S. charonda* (Japan). *Chlorippe* species (see page 55) are in the same group.

35

♂

Scientific name	*Chlorippe cherubina*
Family	Nymphalidae
Common name	None
Wingspan	6–7 cm.
Range	Venezuela, Colombia, Ecuador, Peru, Bolivia, upper Amazon area.
Habits and habitat	Forest species frequently seen at rotten fruit, excrement or other decaying matter. When not feeding plays high up in the trees.
Food-plants	Celtis species.
Sexual dimorphism	The female lacks the bright blue-green of the male and is instead light brown with a white band.
Subspecies and similar species	*Chlorippe* is closely related to the genus *Apaturinidae.* Similar to the above is *C. seraphina* from southern Brazil and Colombia. There are several other species in the genus but none has such a large blue area over the wings: most others are rather dull in comparison.

36

under side ♀

Scientific name	*Dione vanillae*
Family	Nymphalidae
Common name	Gulf Fritillary or Silver-spotted Flambeau
Wingspan	7·5–8·0 cm.
Range	A very large range from southern North America and the West Indies, through Central America, and South America as far south as Buenos Aires.
Habits and habitat	Found almost anywhere, often feeding from flowers. Flies all year round and is almost continuously brooded. This species is migratory. Fast in flight but often settles and then easy to catch.
Food-plants	Passiflorae (passion-flowers) such as P. foetida.
Sexual dimorphism	The female's upper side is darker than the male's and with heavier markings and a thick black margin. The upper side of the male virtually lacks the silver spots, and has a dark border.
Subspecies and similar species	There are several similar species, such as *D. juno, D. moneta,* and many forms of the above species, which is extremely variable.

37

♂

Scientific name	*Terinos terpander*
Family	Nymphalidae
Common name	Royal Assyrian
Wingspan	7 cm.
Range	Confined to Malaysia.
Habits and habitat	A species of the forest, it flutters along weakly, often out into roads, or may be found in rocky places and quarries. A lowland species. Often settles on trees to rest. Drinks at damp patches.
Food-plants	Antidesma.
Sexual dimorphism	The female is very similar but with less blue.
Subspecies and similar species	Similar are *T. alurgis* and a number of other species. There are several subspecies of *T. terpander*.

38

♂

Scientific name	*Catonephele numilia*
Family	Nymphalidae
Common name	Grecian Shoemaker
Wingspan	7·0–7·5 cm.
Range	Mexico, all Central America, South America as far south as Paraguay and Uruguay.
Habits and habitat	Found in jungle areas, flying around tops of trees, but does emerge to feed at refuse, rotting fruit, even coming close to habitation. Frequently seen with Catagramma and Callicore species.
Food-plants	Alchornia iricura, Cordata, Citharayxlum fruticosum.
Sexual dimorphism	The female is larger, with yellow on the fore wings, no blue, and an area of rusty-red on the hind wings.
Subspecies and similar species	There are several similar species marked with golden-orange and others lacking the blue. Best known is *C. aconitus.*

39

♂

Scientific name	*Parthenos sylvia*
Family	Nymphalidae
Common name	Clipper
Wingspan	10 cm.
Range	India, Ceylon, Assam, Burma, Laos, Vietnam, Thailand, Cambodia, Malaysia, Borneo, Sumatra, Java, Celebes, Moluccas, New Guinea, Solomon Islands.
Habits and habitat	A lowland jungle species, common at forest edges and in scrub areas; may soar high over trees or feed at flowers. Drinks at rivulets, often congregating in numbers. Comes near to villages. Found from 1,000 to 3,000 feet. Flies all year round.
Food-plants	Cucurbitaceae vines, Modecca (Passifloraceae), Adenia palmata, Tinospora cordifolia.
Sexual dimorphism	The sexes are almost identical.
Subspecies and similar species	There are many slightly varying forms in the range of *P. sylvia*. Illustrated is the form *P. sylvia lilacinus* from the Malay Peninsula. Similar are a few species such as *P. cyaneus* from Ceylon.

40

41

40 upper side ♀   41 under side ♂

Scientific name	*Dynastor napolean*
Family	Brassolidae
Common name	None
Wingspan	Males 12·5–13·5 cm.
	Females 14·0–16·0 cm.
Range	Only found in São Paulo, Santa Catarina and Rio Grande do Sul areas of Brazil.
Habits and habitat	Little known of this forest species other than that it flies at dusk.
Food-plants	Probably a species of Bromeliaceae.
Sexual dimorphism	The sexes are very similar, except the female is very much larger than the male, as shown in the illustrations.
Subspecies and similar species	The above is a fascinating species from an archaic genus.
	There are other species in the genus, such as *D. darius,* but none spectacular.

42

♂

Scientific name	*Dasyopthalma rusina*
Family	Brassolidae
Common name	None
Wingspan	8–9 cm.
Range	Only found in Santa Catarina province of Brazil.
Habits and habitat	Little-known, but found in low-lying forest areas, especially along river courses. Flies all year round and only in the very early morning or early evening.
Food-plants	Probably feeds on bamboo.
Sexual dimorphism	Sexes very similar: the female has perhaps less blue.
Subspecies and similar species	The race illustrated is *D. rusina principersa*. There are other species in the genus but these are very dull in colour.

43

♂

Scientific name	*Caligo martia*
Family	Brassolidae
Common name	An 'Owl' butterfly
Wingspan	12–13 cm.
Range	Only found in the Rio Grande do Sul, Santa Catarina and Parana provinces of Brazil.
Habits and habitat	Found only singly and rarely comes to bait, but does feed on sap. On the wing September and October. Generally keeps within the dense jungle and only flies late in the afternoon and into early evening after sunset, and sometimes in the very early morning. Lowland species seen near river valleys up to 1,000 feet.
Food-plants	The life-history is unknown.
Sexual dimorphism	The female is generally rather larger than the male, the blue area on the hind wing does not cover so large an area; there is more white on the fore wings, especially the apical spots, and the borders of the wings are whitish.
Subspecies and similar species	There are few *Caligo* with the same brilliant blue; though species of this genus are considerable in number, none are really similar to the above.

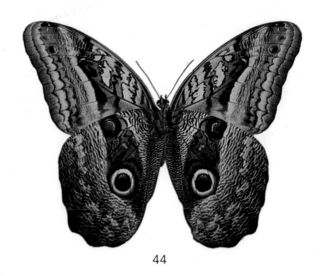

44

underside ♀

Scientific name	*Caligo oileus*
Family	Brassolidae
Common name	An 'Owl' butterfly
Wingspan	16–17 cm.
Range	Mexico, all Central America, Venezuela, Colombia Ecuador, Peru, Bolivia.
Habits and habitat	Only found in dense low-lying forests, sometimes emerging to feed at rotting fruit, especially bananas. Rarely flies in the day-time, sometimes in the early morning, but normally at dusk and later. Often feeds on tree-sap. Can be baited. Flies all year round.
Food-plants	The life-history is unknown.
Sexual dimorphism	Sexes very similar. The upper side of this species is rather dull marked in browns and ochres over the ground colour. On the hind wings especially there is a bluish suffusion.
Subspecies and similar species	The species illustrated is *C. oileus umbratilis* from Peru; there are other named races throughout the area. There are many *Caligo* species that are hard to identify, only a few having rich iridescent blue upper sides.

45

♂

Scientific name	*Morpho hecuba*
Family	Morphidae
Common name	Brown Morpho
Wingspan	14–18 cm.
Range	A species from the Amazon region stretching into the Guianas, Venezuela, Colombia, Ecuador, Peru, Bolivia; does not extend far north in Brazil, the range being defined by the forest lowlands.
Habits and habitat	Found in river valleys or jungle clearings. In most areas flies all year round, this species is known to fly fast over considerable distances. In the lower Amazon the season is very short, only June and July and again in December and January. The butterfly is most common after heavy rains (when adults obviously emerge), but specimens are almost ruined within a very few days. Normally flies high over the tree tops. Fond of fallen fruit, and can be baited.
Food-plants	The life-history is unknown.
Sexual dimorphism	The sexes are very similar; the female is usually larger and paler in colour.
Subspecies and similar species	This species is variable and there are a number of named races. The form illustrated is *M. hecuba obidonus,* found only in the Lower Amazon. This is the largest of all *Morphos* and there are no very similar species, except perhaps the much smaller and duller *M. perseus form Metellus.*

65

46

♂

Scientific name	*Morpho catenarius*
Family	Morphidae
Common name	Green Morpho
Wingspan	12·5–14·5 cm.
Range	Found only in South Brazil from São Paulo to Santa Catarina provinces.
Habits and habitat	This is not a thick forest species. It is found in the underwood near rivers or along paths, and even into habitation. Flying February to April on very hot sunny days in a very lazy fashion. Sometimes comes down to bait.
Food-plants	Inga semialta. The larvae are very conspicuous when feeding in silk webs in groups of twenty to thirty.
Sexual dimorphism	The female is very similar to the male but has more brown spotting on the under side (see also notes below). Also larger than the male.
Subspecies and similar species	The only similar species is *M. laertes,* a pale greenish-blue species from further north. The female of the above has several striking forms: female form marmorata is darker and more heavily marked, female form nigricans is very heavily marked on the under side; neither form is rare, they are regularly found in Santa Catarina.

47

♂

Scientific name	*Morpho achillaena violaceus*
Family	Morphidae
Common name	Violet-Blue Morpho
Wingspan	Male 13·5–14·5 cm.
	Female 14·5–16·0 cm.
Range	Only found in the provinces of São Paulo, Santa Catarina and Rio Grande do Sul in Brazil.
Habits and habitat	This species is confined to the lowlands and mountain foothills. Found in shady areas within the forests especially in damp places. Sometimes drinks at wet patches; not attracted to bait but rarely flies either high or very far. Often seen near the coastline.
Food-plants	The larvae live singly or in very small numbers on Platymiscium and other leguminous plants.
Sexual dimorphism	The female is larger, with blue less intense, all markings larger and more prominent. Additional rows of white spots on fore wings on outside of blue band.
Subspecies and similar species	*M. achilles* is blue instead of violet-blue, and comes from all over the tropical regions of South America. *M. achillaena,* forms are found in central and south Brazil, but the above is the only violet-blue species. Rather similar is *M. deidamia,* which does not extend as far south. There are many named races of *M. achilles and M. achillaena.*

48

♂

Scientific name	*Morpho aega*
Family	Morphidae
Common name	A 'Blue Morpho'
Wingspan	9–10 cm.
Range	Brazil only, from Espírito Santo south through São Paulo and Parana to Santa Catarina.
Habits and habitat	Like all Morphos, found in open places in the forest which are exposed to the hot sun. Frequently seen along roads leading into the forest or along courses of smaller rivers. Females keep to the undergrowth and never fly far.
Food-plants	Life-history unknown.
Sexual dimorphism	The female is quite unlike the male; the common form is cinnamon-coloured, with brown veins and a row of yellowish spots along the borders (form bisanthe). There are in addition two other female forms with varying amounts of blue diffusion on the upper side, the most extreme being almost entirely blue over the light-brown ground colour (form pseudocypris).
Subspecies and similar species	Similar but larger are *M. adonis* and *M. aurora*.

49

♂

Scientific name	*Morpho portis*
Family	Morphidae
Common name	Sky-Blue Morpho
Wingspan	8·9—9·5 cm.
Range	Found only in the Santa Catarina and Rio Grande do Sul provinces of Brazil, and extending into Uruguay.
Habits and habitat	Found in the forest regions, especially where bamboo grows, and where the area is divided by large rivers. Flies generally in mid-afternoon, slowly and low over the ground. Often resting with closed wings on bamboo. Flies high up in damp woods and valleys in higher regions. In some areas there are two broods per season, in the spring and the autumn.
Food-plants	The life-history is unknown.
Sexual dimorphism	The female is similar but with a much wider brown border to all wings; also paler, almost pinkish blue.
Subspecies and similar species	The illustration is of the race *M. portis thamyris;* other races are named but they differ little from the above.

50

♂

Scientific name	*Morpho anaxibia*
Family	Morphidae
Common name	A 'Blue Morpho'
Wingspan	15–16 cm.
Range	Brazil from Espírito Santo province south through São Paulo, and Santa Catarina to Rio Grande do Sul.
Habits and habitat	Flies from the end of January to early March, always singly. Males may gather in the vicinity of waterfalls. Always a species of the lowland forests, found in clearings or along tracks.
Food-plants	Canella and Myrtaceae.
Sexual dimorphism	The female is very distinctive, with a wide dark border to all wings, a white spot in the fore wings, and spots of pinkish or white or yellow within the border. The blue is also much darker.
Subspecies and similar species	*M. anaxibia* may be described as being midway between the Menelaus and the Rhetenor group of Morphos.

51

♂

Scientific name	*Morpho rhetenor*
Family	Morphidae
Common name	A 'Blue Morpho'
Wingspan	13–15 cm.
Range	Venezuela, Guianas, lower Amazon area of Brazil.
Habits and habitat	The males are known to smell of sulphur. A jungle species often flying into the open although generally high up. Flies all year round—the seasons are rather indefinite—from 11 a.m. onwards. The females always keep well within the forest; the males will be found in sunny clearings or other places exposed to the hot sun. Can be lured or baited.
Food-plants	The life-history is unknown.
Sexual dimorphism	The female is not blue but entirely coloured in shades of brown, ochre and yellow on the upper side. There is also an extremely rare form with blue on the upper wings of the female.
Subspecies and similar species	The form illustrated is *M. rhetenor rhetenor* from the Guianas, also named is *M. rhetenor eusebes* from the lower Amazon area, which is larger. From the same family is *M. rhetenor helena*, although this is easily distinguished from the above by the white band (see page 74).

53

52

52 ♂   53 ♀

Scientific name	*Morpho menelaus*
Family	Morphidae
Common name	A 'Blue Morpho'
Wingspan	13–14 cm.
Range	West Colombia, Venezuela, Guianas, east and south Brazil as far south as Santa Catarina province.
Habits and habitat	Found in the jungle, they love fallen fruit and often fly out into the open. They fly all year round, the seasons being irregular, from early morning to nearly midday in the hot sun. Found in clearings, openings into the wood or at hill tops, frequently flying over the tree tops.
Food-plants	The life-history is completely unknown.
Sexual dimorphism	The female, as illustrated, is quite different from the male.
Subspecies and similar species	There are several named races of this species all being rather similar except *M. menelaus nestira* from Santa Catarina, which is a huge race with its upper side like *M. didius*; all have the characteristic *M. menelaus* under side. Similar except for its much greater size is *M. didius* from Peru and part of Bolivia; also similar are *M. amathonte* and *M. godarti*.

54

♂

Scientific name	*Morpho rhetenor helena*
Family	Morphidae
Common name	A 'Blue Morpho'
Wingspan	14·5–15·5 cm.
Range	Only found in the Tingo Maria to Tarapoto area of Peru.
Habits and habitat	Generally soaring high over the trees in thick forests, this species does feed on fallen fruit and can be baited. Always seen in the hot sun, coming into the open in clearings.
Food-plants	The life-history is unknown.
Sexual dimorphism	The female is ochreous-yellow and brown.
Subspecies and similar species	The above is a subspecies (or possible geographic race) of *M. rhetenor* (see page 71); it is similar on the upper side to *M. cipris* (see page 75), although with only a single white band.

55

♂

Scientific name	*Morpho cipris*
Family	Morphidae
Common name	A 'Blue Morpho'
Wingspan	13–14 cm.
Range	Nicaragua, Costa Rica, Panama, Colombia and north-west Venezuela.
Habits and habitat	Found only at great height in forest clearings. Nothing else is known of this superb butterfly.
Food-plants	Life-history unknown.
Sexual dimorphism	The female is quite unlike the male, being yellowish-brown.
Subspecies and similar species	This species is similar (plus the additional white band), to *M. rhetenor helena,* although perhaps the blue is even more intense and it may be said to replace the latter in this part of South America. Female form cyanites is blue (viz. *M. aega form pseudocypris)* but is exceedingly rare.

56

♂

Scientific name	*Thauria aliris*
Family	Amathusidae
Common name	Tufted Jungle King.
Wingspan	11 cm.
Range	Southern Burma, Thailand, Malaysia, Borneo.
Habits and habitat	Flies in thick forest just before sunset. Two broods per season. Feeds on rotting fruit and even found close to habitation on refuse and decaying matter. Found both on the plains and in mountain areas. The female hardly ever seen, keeping to the darkest forest near the breeding ground.
Food-plants	Probably species of bamboo and palm.
Sexual dimorphism	Sexes very similar but the female lacks the tufts of hair on either side of the abdomen.
Subspecies and similar species	Very similar is the rare Indian *T. lathyi,* which may well prove to be only a subspecies of the above.

57

♂

Scientific name	*Thaumantis diores*
Family	Amathusidae
Common name	Jungle Glory
Wingspan	10–11 cm.
Range	Sikkim, Bhutan, Assam, Burma, Yunnan area of China, North Vietnam, Hainan Island.
Habits and habitat	This species only flies from dusk or later. A forest species, but it frequently comes out to feed at refuse, rotten fruit and other decaying matter, even entering habitation. A lowland species only seen up to 4,000 feet (in the north of India) where it flies in May and again in September.
Food-plants	Life-history unknown: probably a palm.
Sexual dimorphism	Sexes very similar, but the female is larger and with the blue areas less bright and more diffused.
Subspecies and similar species	Similar is *T. noureddin* from the same area and *T. lucipor* from Malaysia. Also similar is the genus Zeuxidia (mostly in Malaysia).

58

59

58 upper side ♂   59 under side ♂

Scientific name	*Sticopthalma camadeva*
Family	Amathusidae
Common name	Northern Jungle Queen
Wingspan	12–13 cm.
Range	Sikkim, Bhutan, Assam, northern Burma.
Habits and habitat	A forest species, flying close to the ground in dense vegetation. One brood in north India, May to July. Often met with in clearings. Attracted to over-ripe fruit. Flies between 2,000 and 3,000 feet.
Food-plants	Species of bamboo and palm.
Sexual dimorphism	Sexes identical.
Subspecies and similar species	The illustration is of *S. camadeva camadevoides* from Assam and northern Burma. The type form is found in Sikkim. Similar are *S. howqua*, *S. sparta* and *S. nourmahal.*

60

♂

Scientific name	*Diorina periander*
Family	Riodinidae
Common name	Blue Doctor
Wingspan	4·0–4·5 cm.
Range	From Honduras through central America, and South America as far south as Paraguay and Uruguay.
Habits and habitat	Found in open places, forest clearings, wood edges, often at wet stones or damp patches in the road in the early morning. Plays around shrubs and trees when hot and sunny. Loves both water and decaying matter, and can be baited. Often sits on the under sides of leaves. Flies off to circle around and return to the same spot. Also feeds at flowers. Flies all year round.
Food-plants	The life-history is unknown.
Sexual dimorphism	The female is white, banded in double rows across the wings, and lacks the blue colouring of the male.
Subspecies and similar species	There are many other species of Diorina, such as *D. arcius.* The species are all rather difficult to identify.

61

under side ♂

Scientific name	*Ancyluris meliboeus*
Family	Riodinidae
Common name	None
Wingspan	4·5–5·5 cm.
Range	Guianas, Venezuela, Colombia, Ecuador, Peru, Bolivia, and all of the Amazon region of Brazil.
Habits and habitat	Found in scrub and woodland, often circling around the tops of high bushes. In the early morning comes down to drink at wet patches. Frequently several seen together on flowering shrubs, but always local.
Food-plants	Life-history unknown.
	Note: descriptions below apply to the upper surface, which is a dark ground colour with narrow vivid pink-red band across fore wings and hind wings, plus an extra mark in the short tail, overall dark blue sheen.
Sexual dimorphism	The female's upper side is much duller in colour, with thinner bands and less red, besides being larger and with more rounded wings; under side is similar in both sexes.
Subspecies and similar species	This is an extremely variable species with numerous named races. Illustrated is *A. meliboeus rubrofilum* from Peru and Bolivia. There are many other similar species in the same genus; the best known is *A. formosissima*.

62   63

62 ♂   63 ♀

Scientific name	*Heodes virguareae*
Family	Lycaenidae
Common name	Scarce Copper
Wingspan	3·0–3·5 cm.
Range	Europe (but not Britain or north France) north to the Arctic Circle, Asia Minor, and central Asia to Mongolia.
Habits and habitat	Flies in meadows, woods, mountain-sides and flowery slopes. Found up to 10,000 feet, but usually a lowland species from June to August. Loves flowers especially thyme. Keeps near the ground. Always a local species. One brood per season.
Food-plants	Rumex, Solidago.
Sexual dimorphism	The female is, as illustrated, rather dull compared with the male.
Subspecies and similar species	There are many named races of the above which varies greatly throughout its range. There are several similar species such as *H. ottomanus* and *H. thetis.* Also in the group are the races of *L. dispar* once found as a race in Britain (now the Dutch race has been introduced).

64   65

64 ♂   65 ♀

Scientific name	*Lysandra bellargus*
Family	Lycaenidae
Common name	Adonis Blue
Wingspan	3–5 cm.
Range	South and central Europe (including southern England) up to about 55° north. In the east from Latvia in north as far south as Iran and Iraq.
Habits and habitat	Found in open places, rough ground, sunny slopes, but always on calcareous ground. Rests on small plants such as scabious, thistles and grass stalks. Occurs up to 7,000 feet. Usually two broods in May to June and again in August to September.
Food-plants	Hippocrepis, Coronilla and various small Leguminosae.
Sexual dimorphism	The female is very variable, sometimes with large orange lunules and less often almost completely suffused with blue (form ceronus).
Subspecies and similar species	Only the under side of many of the Lycaenids are similar, but on the upper side only the following have a fairly similar colouring: *P. escheri* and *L. punctifera.*

66

♂

Scientific name	*Ornithoptera helena*
Family	Papilionidae
Common name	Common Birdwing
Wingspan	Males 13–15 cm.
	Females 16–18 cm.
Range	Sikkim, Bhutan, Assam, India, Ceylon, Burma, south-east China, Vietnam, Thailand, Laos, Malaysia, Borneo, Sumatra, Java, Celebes, Moluccas, New Guinea.
Habits and habitat	A forest species, they fly around tree tops, but also settle on flowering trees. Found in clearings and along paths, often coming into villages. Normally they do not drink at wet places. Fly early in the morning and descend again in the evening. Up to 3,000 feet in north India, and except for this area they fly all year round.
Food-plants	Aristolochia indica, and other Aristolochia, and Bragantia wallichii species.
Sexual dimorphism	The female is much larger than the male, having huge black spots on the hind wings, like the female O. aecus (page 85), but much darker ground colour and spotting; the yellow is brighter.
Subspecies and similar species	Similar are *O. aecus, O. magellanus, O. amphrysus* and others. *O. helena* has numerous named and varied subspecies. Illustrated is *O. helena cerberus* (from north India to Malaysia). Other subspecies are very different, females being very black spotted or banded on the hind wings.

67

♀

Scientific name	*Ornithoptera aecus*
Family	Papilionidae
Common name	Golden Birdwing
Wingspan	Males 13–15 cm.
	Females 16–18 cm.
Range	Sikkim, Bhutan, Assam, into Tibet, south-east China, Taiwan.
Habits and habitat	Flies high up on sunny days, often visiting flowers, or descending to drink at damp sand. Normally found in foothills between 800 and 3,500 feet, in forested valleys. In India flies May to September.
Food-plants	Aristolochia indica, other species of Aristolochia, Bragantia wallichii. Larvae gregarious when young.
Sexual dimorphism	The male is smaller than the female and does not have the black spots on the hind wings. Like the male O. helena (see page 84), but less bright, yellow duller, ground colour brown, and like the female has greyish white dusting around the veins on the fore wings.
Subspecies and similar species	Similar are *O. helena, O. amphrysus, O. magellanus, O. rhadamanthus* and many others. There is a very large group of commonly named 'Black' and 'Yellow' Birdwings.

68

69

68 ♂   69 ♀

Scientific name	*Ornithoptera brookiana*
Family	Papilionidae
Common name	Rajah Brooke's Birdwing
Wingspan	Males 16–18 cm.
	Females 17–19 cm.
Range	West and east Malaysia, Borneo, Palawan, Sumatra.
Habits and habitat	Strictly a jungle species, although often comes very close to inhabited areas. Fond of flowers and moist places, and especially hot springs. Loves decaying matter and often seen at rubbish and dung. At lower elevations below 3,500 feet. Frequently the males will gather to feed in dozens. The females fly higher in the hills, often 30 feet up in the flowering trees, still on the wing in the early evening. Both sexes do descend to ground level, but only in the early morning.
Food-plants	Species of Aristolochia, Apama corymbosa.
Sexual dimorphism	As shown, the sexes are quite different. The markings of the female vary, often with far more white on the fore wings and wing-tips.
Subspecies and similar species	There are only two well-known races of this butterfly: illustrated is *O. brookiana albescens* (the Malayan form); the other is *O. brookiana trogon* from Sumatra, Borneo, and the east of the area, this race is rarer and never congregates at damp to drink.

87

70

♂

Scientific name	*Ornithoptera priamus urvillianus*
Family	Papilionidae
Common name	Blue Birdwing
Wingspan	Males 16–18 cm.
	Females 19–21 cm.
Range	Only found in the Solomon Isles group.
Habits and habitat	Entirely a jungle species found from sea level to 2,000 feet, especially in the vicinity of rivers. The female will feed at flowers, coming out into the open, but the male generally keeps high up in the trees. Generally flying December to April, but does breed all year round.
Food-plants	Aristolochia tagala and other Aristolochia species.
Sexual dimorphism	The female is quite unlike the male: instead she is brownish marked with large patches of greyish-white and similarly on the hind wing, and she is very much larger.
Subspecies and similar species	Throughout its range this species has many forms, the more extreme becoming not blue but blue-green. Also in the same group are *O. p. poseidon* (green) and *O. p. croesus* (orange).

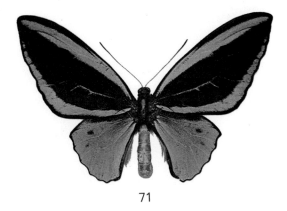

71

♂

Scientific name	*Ornithoptera priamus poseidon*
Family	Papilionidae
Common name	New Guinea or Green Birdwing
Wingspan	Males 16–18 cm.
	Females 19–21 cm.
Range	Moluccas, New Guinea, Queensland and New South Wales in Australia, plus many islands in the area.
Habits and habitat	Jungle species flying high except in the early morning or late afternoon. Very fond of hibiscus, poinsettia and bougainvillaea. Can be lured.
	Flies all year round except in Australia where it has two or three broods in its season. Males often found in open places; the females keep more in the trees. Both sexes may be caught while at flowers.
Food-plants	Aristolochia (Dutchman's pipe): A. deltantha, A. parvenosa, A. indica, A. elegens, A. tagala. Also probably Magnifolia indica.
Sexual dimorphism	The female is not like the male; she is similar to all other priamus females, brown marked with greyish-white and with or without a band of yellowish colour on the hind wings; she is very much larger than the male.
Subspecies and similar species	The type *O. priamus* (as above but much larger) comes from Amboina, Saparoea and Seram. The illustrated species is from New Guinea and the Torres Isles. There are three races in Australia.
	No doubt of the same origin as the above are the blue and orange species (*O. priamus urvillianus* and *O. priamus croesus*).

72

♂

Scientific name	*Ornithoptera priamus croesus*
Family	Papilionidae
Common name	Orange Birdwing
Wingspan	Males 16–20 cm.
	Females 20–25 cm.
Range	In the Moluccas and Halmahera, Batjan, and other small islands in the area.
Habits and habitat	A species of the jungles, can be found at low elevations but always rather inaccessible. Normally flies very high.
Food-plants	Life-history unknown.
Sexual dimorphism	The female is similar to the others in the same group, being of a plain grey-brown colour, but on the under side has more light areas, and the yellow is lighter and more extensive. This yellow shows through on the upper side making it far more attractive than the other plain females in the group.
Subspecies and similar species	Very similar is *O. priamus lydius,* from Halmahera and Ternate which is orange in colour and does not have the greenish sheen. The above is in the same group as the blue *O. p. urvillianus* and the green *O. p. poseidon.*

73

♂

Scientific name	*Schoenbergia paradisea*
Family	Papilionidae
Common name	Tailed Birdwing
Wingspan	Males 17 cm.
	Females 22 cm.
Range	New Guinea only, fairly scattered, but generally in the area of the Finisterre Mountains.
Habits and habitat	Found in mountainside ravines in forest areas at about 1,500 feet. Visits flowers, coming down in early morning or late afternoon. Continuously brooded. Normally flies high above the trees, only coming down to feed or to lay.
Food-plants	Aristolochia species. Given a large flight area, could probably be easily reared.
Sexual dimorphism	The female is quite unlike the male and is larger greyish black in colour: the fore wings have two rows of white spots; the hind wings are yellowish around the border, shading inwards to bluish grey and off-white.
Subspecies and similar species	Similar is *S. meridionalis,* with smaller and less developed tail. There are two named sub-species of *S. paradisea:* subspecies *flavescens* and subspecies *arfakensis*—both much rarer than the above.

74

75

74 ♂   75 ♀

Scientific name	*Schoenbergia goliath*
Family	Papilionidae
Common name	Goliath Birdwing
Wingspan	Males 18–22 cm.
	Females 25–28 cm.
Range	The various races occur in different parts of New Guinea, Seram and Moluccas.
Habits and habitat	Little is known of this species: it is found in the very thick and inaccessible jungle forests and deep valleys, and is very difficult to collect due to the thickness of the jungle and the terrain.
Food-plants	Life-history not known.
Sexual dimorphism	The female is typically unlike the male, as illustrated.
Subspecies and similar species	There are no very similar species. Several races of this butterfly have been named; our illustration is of *S. goliath supremus.* As in most Birdwings this species varies both in colour and markings. The female of the above has probably the largest wing area of any known butterfly (but female *O. alexandrae* may be a little larger).

76

♂

Scientific name	*Papilio antimachus*
Family	Papilionidae
Common name	African Giant Swallowtail
Wingspan	Males 20–23 cm.
	Females 15 cm.
Range	Sierra Leone, Guinea, Ivory Coast, Ghana, Nigeria, Cameroons, Central African Republic, Gabon, the two Congos, west Uganda.
Habits and habitat	The male sometimes comes down to drink at water, whereas the female always remains within the thick forest. Generally the male flies very fast and high up.
Food-plants	Life history and food-plants unknown.
Sexual dimorphism	The female is smaller and more round-winged than the male.
Subspecies and similar species	There is no similar species. The above resembles a giant butterfly of the Acraea genus and early lepidopterists did not consider it a Papilionid.

77

♂

Scientific name	*Papilio zalmoxis*
Family	Papilionidae
Common name	Giant Blue Swallowtail
Wingspan	15·5–18·5 cm.
Range	West Cameroon (into Nigeria), Central African Republic, Guinea, Gabon, the Congos, West Uganda.
Habits and habitat	Confined to the forest regions, often found drinking at mud. Flies all year round: some years in number, other years hardly any at all.
Food-plants	Life-history entirely unknown.
Sexual dimorphism	The female has greyish-blue hind wings with a yellowish colour in the cell of the fore wing.
Subspecies and similar species	None.

78

♂

Scientific name	*Papilio zagreus*
Family	Papilionidae
Common name	None
Wingspan	12–13 cm.
Range	Venezuela, Colombia, Ecuador, Peru, Bolivia.
Habits and habitat	Little is known of this species. It flies singly in high mountain areas, often within the forest.
Food-plants	Nothing is known of the life-history of this species.
Sexual dimorphism	Sexes very similar, the female is lighter in colour.
Subspecies and similar species	Similar are *P. bachus* (Colombia to Bolivia and Peru) and also *P. ascolias* (Panama to West Ecuador and Colombia). *P. zagreus* is a very variable species.

79

♂

Scientific name	Papilio sesostris
Family	Papilionidae
Common name	Southern Cattle Heart
Wingspan	Males 10–11 cm. Females 11–12 cm.
Range	Mexico, Central America, Colombia, Venezuela, Guianas, Ecuador, Peru, Bolivia, the entire area of the Amazon region of Brazil.
Habits and habitat	Confined to forest areas, sometimes emerging along tracks or into clearings. Feeds at flowers sometimes in number.
Food-plants	Aristolochia (probably A. grandiflora and others).
Sexual dimorphism	Only the male has the scent organ in the folds on the inner border of the hind wings. The female is black with two large, off-white spots on the fore wings, and a partial wide pink-red band across the hind wings.
Subspecies and similar species	There are a number of different races of this species; the most common does not have the red spot on the hind wings in the male. Illustrated is *P. sesostris zestos*. Similar are many species within this group of swallowtails.

80

♂

Scientific name	*Papilio neophilus*
Family	Papilionidae
Common name	Spear Winged Cattle Heart
Wingspan	Male 8·5–9·5 cm.
	Female 9–10 cm.
Range	Venezuela, Trinidad, Guianas, Colombia, Ecuador, Peru, Bolivia, Paraguay, all of Brazil except the most eastern coastal sector.
Habits and habitat	Forest species, avoiding the sunshine. Flies after rainstorms. Frequently settles on undergrowth and may be found along paths or near rivers in thick trees. In lowlands and mountain foothills areas. Found all year round.
Food-plants	Aristolochia trilobata and other species of Aristolochia.
Sexual dimorphism	The female is quite unlike the male. The fore wings are black with white centres; the hind wings have a band of vivid pink across the wings and the margins are coloured similarly.
Subspecies and similar species	There are several named geographical races of *P. neophilus.* The form illustrated is *P. neophilus ecbolius* (from the Lower Amazon upwards to Obidos). There are great numbers of beautiful species similar to the above, some pink and white, others red and green, etc.

81

♂

Scientific name	*Papilio nireus*
Family	Papilionidae
Common name	Blue-banded Swallowtail
Wingspan	9–12 cm.
Range	Covers a large area of Africa, from Sierra Leone to Kenya in the north of the range and through all countries south to the Cape of South Africa.
Habits and habitat	A species found in forest, bush, savannah, and virtually everywhere, even into gardens. Flies all year round, except in the south where it is on the wing September to April. Feeds on flowers.
Food-plants	Citrus, Fagara, Teclea, Vepris, Toddalia, Calodendron capensis, Clausena inequalis, and other species of Rutaceae.
Sexual dimorphism	In the female the band is greenish, and on the under side is mottled in silvery-brown and without the whitish stripe on the hind wing.
Subspecies and similar species	There are more than seven similar species. The race from southern Africa is *P. nireus lyaeus* with a narrower band. Similar are *P. sosia, P. bromius, P. magdae,* and several other less common species.

82

♂

Scientific name	*Papilio demoleus*
Family	Papilionidae
Common name	Lime Butterfly or Chequered Swallowtail
Wingspan	8–10 cm.
Range	Iran (into Syria), Afghanistan, India, Pakistan, Ceylon, Burma, southern China to Taiwan, Vietnam, Thailand, Malaysia, Sumatra, Java, Borneo, New Guinea, Australia (not on Celebes, Moluccas or Philippines).
Habits and habitat	Flies all year round in tropical localities, but in the cool north has only one brood a year. Common in meadow and field as well as in the forest, often feeding at flowers, frequently coming into gardens and orchards. This lowland species often collect together in large numbers, sometimes at damp patches. Found up to 7,000 feet in the Himalayas, but usually below 2,000 feet.
Food-plants	Fruit trees, especially lime and orange (citrus). Also Feronia elephantum, Aegle marmelos, Zizyphus jujuba, Glycosmis pentaphylla, Salvia sub-species, Psoralea tenax, Ruta graveolens.
Sexual dimorphism	Sexes virtually identical: the female is perhaps a little paler in colour.
Subspecies and similar species	Very similar, and often classified as the same species, is *P. demodocus* from Africa; no doubt they both developed from one species.

83

♂

Scientific name	*Papilio thyastes*
Family	Papilionidae
Common name	None
Wingspan	9–11 cm.
Range	Ecuador, Peru, Bolivia, Brazil, Mexico to Honduras and Guatemala.
Habits and habitat	Although females never come out of the forest, the males are found in sunny open places around the edges of woods or within the clearings. Males visit flowers and often congregate at streams, rivers or wet places to drink water.
Food-plants	The life-history is unknown.
Sexual dimorphism	Sexes probably identical.
Subspecies and similar species	There are several rather similar species which are rarely seen.

84

♂

Scientific name	*Papilio protesilaus*
Family	Papilionidae
Common name	Northern White Page
Wingspan	9·5–10·5 cm.
Range	Mexico, Guatemala, Honduras, Nicaragua, Costa Rica, Panama, Colombia, Venezuela, Guianas, Ecuador, Peru, Bolivia, Brazil.
Habits and habitat	The males may often be seen on damp sand or mud in clusters. Males visit flowers and love the sun, being found in forest clearings or near woods; the females keep within the interior. Sometimes males are found at mountain tops or on long flights over the trees. Generally a lowland species.
Food-plants	Life-history not known.
Sexual dimorphism	The female is very similar to the male, but usually larger. The male has a small scent gland on the hind wings.
Subspecies and similar species	There are several similar species that are often hard to distinguish one from another, e.g. *P. agesilaus, P. telesilaus, P. autosilaus,* etc.

85

♂

Scientific name	*Papilio weiskei*
Family	Papilionidae
Common name	Purple-Spotted Swallowtail
Wingspan	8·0–8·5 cm.
Range	Only found in New Guinea, especially in the south-east (Papua), on both sides of the Owen Stanley mountain range.
Habits and habitat	Found in the mountain forest, and rarely descends out of the high trees, where it flies very fast. Descends to feed at flowers in the early morning. Flies all year round.
Food-plants	Life-history not known.
Sexual dimorphism	Both sexes very similar.
Subspecies and similar species	Similar, but without the violet, is *P. macleayanus* (from Australia). The purple-violet colouring does vary in the above.

86

♀

Scientific name	*Papilio philoxenus*
Family	Papilionidae
Common name	Common Windmill
Wingspan	11–13 cm.
Range	Kashmir, Nepal, Sikkim, Bhutan, Assam, Burma, Laos, Vietnam, south-east China, Taiwan.
Habits and habitat	Basically a forest species found between 1,000 and 8,000 feet. Flies all year round, usually high up. Loves flowers, coming out in the open to feed. The females remain hidden. Several broods per season, usually April to October.
Food-plants	Nepenthes.
Sexual dimorphism	The female is very similar to the male, but has much more colour on the hind wings, and is considerably larger.
Subspecies and similar species	Similar are *P. dasarada, P. latreillei, P. aristolochia* and others. There are several named races of the above.

87

♂

Scientific name	*Papilio hector*
Family	Papilionidae
Common name	Crimson Rose
Wingspan	10–12 cm.
Range	Ceylon and all of southern India extending up to Bengal in the east.
Habits and habitat	A species generally confined to the hot lowland areas, found almost anywhere, but very fond of flowering plants and trees (Lantana a favourite). Specimens taken up to 8,000 feet, as partially migratory in Ceylon, but usually only seen below 1,000 feet. Flies all year round. In the autumn large numbers often gather to roost in trees.
Food-plants	Aristolochia indica and sometimes Citrus.
Sexual dimorphism	The female is paler in colour, being almost pinkish, and is larger, with fore wings more rounded, and darker body.
Subspecies and similar species	Similar are *P. philoxenus, P. aristolochiae, P. polytes* and many others, but none is as bright in colour. *P. hector* is a variable species, sometimes having huge crimson spots.

88

♂

Scientific name	*Papilio menestheus*
Family	Papilionidae
Common name	Emperor Swallowtail
Wingspan	10–14 cm.
Range	Sierra Leone, Guinea, Ivory Coast, Ghana, Nigeria, Cameroons, Central African Republic, Gabon, Congo, Congo Republic, Angola, Tanzania, Uganda, west Kenya. Also in Madagascar (Malagasy Republic).
Habits and habitat	Forest species, found on tracks and in clearings. Flies all year round. The male drinks at water and may emerge out of the forest to feed at flowers, but the female rarely appears.
Food-plants	Fagara macrophylla, Citrus, Vepris, Clausena anisata.
Sexual dimorphism	Sexes very similar, the female is usually larger.
Subspecies and similar species	Our illustration is of *P. menestheus lormieri,* the most commonly obtained form (from Gabon, Congo area and Madagascar). The type form is more West African. Similar is *P. ophidicephalus.*

89

♂

Scientific name	*Papilio arcturus*
Family	Papilionidae
Common name	Blue Banded Peacock
Wingspan	12·0–14·0 cm.
Range	Himalayan foothills, Sikkim, Assam to Tenasserim hills in Burma, west and central China, Taiwan.
Habits and habitat	Usually encountered along paths or at openings in wooded areas and on hilltops. Fond of flowers especially Lantana and Hibiscus. Flies all summer from April to October; several broods during the season (two broods in north India). The female is rarely seen. From 5,000 to 10,000 feet.
Food-plants	Fruit trees and Umbelliferae, Aurantiaceae.
Sexual dimorphism	Both sexes similar; the female is usually larger and paler in colour.
Subspecies and similar species	Similar species are *P. hoppo, P. ganesa (polyctor), P. paris* (see page 108), *P. palinurus.*

90

♂

Scientific name	*Papilio paris*
Family	Papilionidae
Common name	Paris Peacock
Wingspan	9–14 cm.
Range	India, Himalayan area, Assam, Burma, south-east China, Taiwan, Thailand, Laos, Vietnam, Sumatra, Java (not in Malaysia or Borneo).
Habits and habitat	Forest areas, clearings, paths, hilltops, usually at lower elevations. Males love flowers especially Lantana and Hibiscus and frequently congregate at damp sand. They often fly continually over a given area. Females rarely seen, preferring the thick forest. Several broods in a season, flying March to October.
Food-plants	Fruit trees (Citrus), and Umbelliferae, Aurantiaceae, Rutaceae, such as Evodia roxburghiana.
Sexual dimorphism	Sexes almost identical; the female is usually larger.
Subspecies and similar species	There are many named forms of this species. The most beautiful is from south India *(P. paris tamile)*, with a huge area of blue-green on the hind wings. The Taiwan race *(P. paris hermosanus)* is very small and rather dull. Similar are *P. ganesa (polyctor), P. arcturus, P. hoppo, P. palinurus*.

91

♂

Scientific name	*Papilio crino*
Family	Papilionidae
Common name	Common Banded Peacock
Wingspan	8·5–10·0 cm.
Range	Ceylon, south India and Calcutta area (? reported also in Cochin Chine in South Vietnam).
Habits and habitat	Generally found on the plains, especially in the spring; also in the hot dry jungle areas, though rarely. Up to 6,000 feet in the mountains of India. Flies all year round. Males congregate at damp sand and also visit flowers. The females fly fast and are hard to catch.
Food-plants	Chloroxylon swietenia (satinwood tree).
Sexual dimorphism	In the female the bands are narrower than in the male.
Subspecies and similar species	Similar are *P. palinurus, P. blumei, P. buddha*, all three being not rare but infrequently collected and very much prized by lepidopterists.

92

♀

Scientific name	*Papilio machaon*
Family	Papilionidae
Common name	Swallowtail
Wingspan	7–10 cm.
Range	Throughout temperate Europe and Asia, from North Africa to the North Cape (Norway), across U.S.S.R., throughout the Mediterranean, all the near eastern countries (Turkey, Persia, etc., but not in Arabia), from Afghanistan into north India, to China and Japan. Also in Canada in the Hudsonian region.
Habits and habitat	A species of the meadows, fields, flowery banks, lowlands and mountains. Males often on hilltops. Frequent also in clearings in sunny woods. In England only found in fen district of Norfolk. Females do not wander far from the breeding ground: sometimes seen drinking at muddy patches in very hot weather. Two broods per year, April/May and July/August, but in the south there may be a third brood in September. Males can be vagrant, but more rarely the females; thus Continental examples come to England, and the species can be found in Canada (arrived, no doubt, from Kamchatka in U.S.S.R.).
Food-plants	Various species of Phellodendron and Umbelliferae, especially the following; Peucedanum palustre (milk parsley), Angelica sylvestris (angelica), Foeniculum vulgare (fennel), Daucus carota (wild carrot), dill. Larvae feed singly but can be reared easily.
Sexual dimorphism	The female is slightly larger than the male; the wings are more rounded but otherwise very similar to the male.
Subspecies and similar species	There are many subspecies of the above that vary in size, markings and colouration. In England there is *P. machaon britannicus,* as illustrated (a wide dark band of blue-black). In Europe the form is *P. m. gorganus.* The spring brood is generally smaller than the summer brood. Similar species are *P. hospiton* and *P. alexanor* in Europe.

93

♂

Scientific name	*Papilio thoas*
Family	Papilionidae
Common name	Giant Yellow Swallowtail
Wingspan	12·5–15·5 cm.
Range	Texas and Mexico, all Central American countries, West Indies, South America as far south as north Argentina and south Brazil.
Habits and habitat	Frequently seen in open places, often appearing in plantations and gardens. Often flies very high in the air. Loves to settle on flowers. Flies all year round except in north.
Food-plants	Piperaceae (Piper marginatum and P. tuberculatum)—these are the candle bush trees. Also on Citrus.
Sexual dimorphism	Sexes are almost identical; the female is slightly larger and paler in colour.
Subspecies and similar species	There are several named subspecies, the type form being more heavily marked and not so bright a yellow; this occurs in Central America and Texas. Illustrated is *P. thoas cinyras* (the South American form). Similar are *P. cresphontes* and *P. lycophron*.

94

♂

Scientific name	*Papilio ulysses*
Family	Papilionidae
Common name	Blue Mountain Butterfly
Wingspan	10·5–14·0 cm.
Range	New Guinea, Moluccas, Queensland (Australia), Bismarck Isles, Solomon Isles, New Hebrides, New Caledonia, and many other islands in the area.
Habits and habitat	A jungle species especially fond of sunny river beds, this butterfly does quite often come out into the open, but normally flies very high. Feeds at flowers, especially Hibiscus, and can be attracted to brightly-coloured lures. Usually at lower altitudes, but up to 3,000 feet in hills. Flies all year round. Perfect examples are rare as this species is attacked in flight by birds.
Food-plants	Evodia accedens, E. elleryana, E. bonwickii (these are corkwood trees), also on Citrus. The larvae feed individually and prefer the young growth.
Sexual dimorphism	Female has less blue area, thinner scaling, and not as bright, with additional blue spots on hind wings; much darker overall.
Subspecies and similar species	Throughout its range this butterfly varies considerably and many subspecies have been named. Similar are *P. montrouzieri* and other rarer species.

95

96

95 ♂   96 ♀

Scientific name	*Teinopalpus imperialis*
Family	Papilionidae
Common name	Kaiser-I-Hind
Wingspan	Males 9·5–10·5 cm.
	Females 11–12 cm.
Range	Nepal, Sikkim, Bhutan, Assam, north-west Burma, into China.
Habits and habitat	Frequents open mountain tops that are surrounded by thick forests. At other times keeps to tree tops, except in the early and mid-morning if it is fine and sunny, when it does descend and can then be attracted to bait. It is always a very fast flier. Found normally between 6,000 and 10,000 feet. Double brooded, flying April to May and again August to September. The male vanishes into the bushes as soon as the sun goes in and is easily taken when hiding.
Food-plants	Daphne nepalensis (Thymeliaceae).
Sexual dimorphism	The sexes are quite different, as shown: the male has only one tail and the female has three tails and is much larger.
Subspecies and similar species	In southern China there is another species, or perhaps a subspecies *T. aureus*; wings more rounded at apex, and yellow areas enlarged.

97

♂

Scientific name	*Armandia lidderdalei*
Family	Papilionidae
Common name	Bhutan Glory
Wingspan	10·5–12·0 cm.
Range	Himalayan area: Kashmir, Nepal, Bhutan, Assam, Burma, into China (Yunnan, Szechwan area); possibly in Tibet.
Habits and habitat	Found at medium and higher elevation from 5,000 to 9,000 feet. A feeble flyer, it floats over tree tops like a falling leaf. Feeds at flowering trees. Hard to see when not flying, as it sits in trees with fore wings completely covering the bright hind wings. Flies from May to June and again from August to September. Two broods per season. On the wing all day long. Delicious odour when alive.
Food-plants	Not known but probably a climbing Aristolochia species.
Sexual dimorphism	Sexes are very similar but the female is usually a little larger and the scarlet is less intense.
Subspecies and similar species	Very similar is the virtually unobtainable *A. thaidina* from China. The above, although not closely related, resembles a giant Thais (Zerynthia) species from southern Europe.

98

♂

Scientific name	*Leptocircus meges*
Family	Papilionidae
Common name	Green Dragontail
Wingspan	4·0–5·5 cm. Note that tails may be 4 cm. in length.
Range	Assam, Naga Hills (India-Burma), south-east China and Hong Kong area, Burma, Laos, Vietnam, Thailand, Cambodia, Malaysia, Sumatra, Java, Borneo, Celebes, Philippines.
Habits and habitat	A jungle species found in open places, especially near streams or rivers, where they dart back and forth like dragonflies in the sunlight. They often settle on the mud and drink water very greedily, squirting it out behind them such is their excess. They love flowers but do not settle, instead hovering with fast quivering wings whilst probing for nectar. Always found singly, they fly in Assam from March to October up to 5,000 feet.
Food-plants	The life-history of this species is unknown.
Sexual dimorphism	Male and female are almost identical; the abdomen of the female is much larger.
Subspecies and similar species	Similar is the White Dragontail *(L. curius)* with a creamy white band instead of a green band. There are several named and slightly varied races of *L. meges* within its area.

99

♂

Scientific name	*Eurema brigitta*
Family	Pieridae
Common name	Broad-Bordered Grass Yellow
Wingspan	4–5 cm.
Range	All Africa south of the Congo area, and in the east into Uganda and Kenya.
Habits and habitat	In open country, bush areas, gardens and plantations. Often congregate in numbers to drink at roadside puddles. Fly all year round.
Food-plants	Hypericum Cassia.
Sexual dimorphism	The female has the bright yellow replaced by a pale yellow and is generally larger, often black dusted.
Subspecies and similar species	Considerable difference is shown between the heavily marked summer form and the winter form that virtually lacks the dark borders. There are a great number of species very similar to the above that may be found in *all* tropical and sub-tropical countries throughout the world. Similar are *E. hecabe* and *E. hapale.*

100

♂

Scientific name	*Prioneris thestylis*
Family	Pieridae
Common name	Spotted Sawtooth
Wingspan	8–9 cm.
Range	Sikkim, Assam, India, Burma, south-east China, Taiwan, Vietnam, Thailand, Malaysia.
Habits and habitat	Found in open country, often gathering in vast numbers at banks or other moist places or at flowers. In India found in mountain valleys up to 4,000 feet. Fly all year round. The female remains mostly within the forest.
Food-plants	Capparis.
Sexual dimorphism	Sexes almost identical.
Subspecies and similar species	This species shows considerable seasonal variation. Illustrated is *P. thestylis malacanna* from the Malay peninsula. Similar are a number of species including *P. clemanthe* and *P. sita.*

101

♂

Scientific name	Delias hyparete
Family	Pieridae
Common name	Painted Jezebel
Wingspan	7·5–8·5 cm.
Range	India, Burma, south-east China, Taiwan, Thailand, Laos, Malaysia, Borneo, Philippines, Celebes.
Habits and habitat	Found in open woods, bush, and even in gardens. Flies all day and often at dusk. Most common at low elevations. Males at flowers or damp patches; females keep in the woods. From 3,000 to 6,000 feet.
Food-plants	Probably Loranthus (mistletoe).
Sexual dimorphism	The sexes are very similar; the female is more heavily dusted with black.
Subspecies and similar species	There are a number of named forms within the region. The illustration is of *D. hyparete hierte* from India. Similar are many species from the Indo-Australian region such as *D. eucharis* and *D. argenthona*.

102

♂

Scientific name	*Delias descombesi*
Family	Pieridae
Common name	Red-Spot Jezebel
Wingspan	4·0–4·5 cm.
Range	Nepal, Sikkim, Assam, south-east China, Burma, Thailand, Cambodia, Malaysia.
Habits and habitat	Found on the plains and up to 7,000 feet. Often wanders into gardens. Weak flyers, they love flowers. Several broods per season. In India fly March to November, and further south all year round.
Food-plants	Loranthus vestitus. Larvae are gregarious. Easy to rear in captivity.
Sexual dimorphism	The female is pale yellow suffused with grey-green on the under side. The upper side of this species is plain white with greyish veins.
Subspecies and similar species	There are several similar Delias species, but none that have the bright yellow hind wings on the under side. Our illustration shows *D. descombesi leucantha* (from Sikkim).

103

♂

Scientific name	*Catopsilia philea*
Family	Pieridae
Common name	Orange-Barred Sulphur.
Wingspan	7·5–8·5 cm.
Range	Mexico, all Central America, all South America as far south as Bolivia and southern Brazil. Recorded also in Texas, Florida and Georgia, but no doubt these are immigrants.
Habits and habitat	A lowland species. The males very often congregate at damp spots and especially river banks in very large numbers; also they are much attracted by sweat and urine; also they feed at flowers. The female usually remains in the tree cover. Flies in hottest sunshine.
Food-plants	Cassia fistula, C. fruticosa.
Sexual dimorphism	The female is unlike the male: there is a row of brown spots on the fore wing and no orange patch; the hind wings have a very wide band of orange, shading to yellow.
Subspecies and similar species	Similar are *C. avellaneda* from Cuba, a superb species splashed with red, *C. argante,* all orange. *C. cipris* and *C. rurina* have two different shades of yellow on the upper side.

104

♂

Scientific name	*Ixias pyrene*
Family	Pieridae
Common name	Yellow Orange Tip
Wingspan	6–8 cm.
Range	India, Ceylon, Assam, East Pakistan, Burma, south-east China, Taiwan, Laos, Thailand, Malaysia, Borneo.
Habits and habitat	Flies in the heat of the day, rapidly from flower to flower. Males congregate at wet places where there is little vegetation. The females visit only flowers and keep to sheltered places in scrub. Rarely above 4,500 feet, this species normally keeps to the hot plains and is common near the sea. Breeds continuously all year round.
Food-plants	Capparis sepieria and other Capparidae.
Sexual dimorphism	The usual female form is rather similar to the male, but having the orange tip split and reduced to but a few large orange dots.
Subspecies and similar species	There are numerous named races and the species shows considerable seasonal variation, as well as being itself most variable. In some races the male has the yellow replaced by off-white; the female may be all yellow or all off-white. There are a number of rather similar species that could easily be confused with races of the above: for example *I. marianne* (from south India and Ceylon).

105

♂

Scientific name	*Appias nero*
Family	Pieridae
Common name	Orange Albatross
Wingspan	7·0–7·5 cm.
Range	Sikkim, Assam, Burma, Laos, Thailand, Malaysia, Borneo, Sumatra, Java, Celebes, Moluccas, Philippines.
Habits and habitat	The males frequent paths in woods, and are sometimes found at puddles or forest streams in large numbers. The females rarely drink but keep to the higher areas of the forest and attend flowering trees.
Food-plants	Capparidae.
Sexual dimorphism	The female is very similar to the male but has a black border to the wing margins and a short black band on the fore wings.
Subspecies and similar species	There are many named subspecies throughout the area. The illustration is of *A. nero figulina* (from the Malay peninsula). There is no similar all-orange butterfly.

106

♂

Scientific name	*Hebomoia glaucippe*
Family	Pieridae
Common name	Great Orange Tip
Wingspan	9–11 cm.
Range	India, Ceylon, southern China to Taiwan, Vietnam, Thailand, Cambodia, Burma, Malaysia, Borneo, Sumatra, Java, Celebes, Moluccas.
Habits and habitat	The males can be seen in the morning along paths and edges of woods and in open thickets. From midday, males frequently congregate on moist sand, especially river banks. Females feed on flowers especially Lantana, and prefer to remain amongst the trees. Males often wander into gardens. A species of both the lowlands and the mountains.
Food-plants	Capparis moonii, Crataeva religiosa and other Capparidae.
Sexual dimorphism	The female is larger than the male, with a series of black spots on the hind wings. The orange tip is duller. In some races the female ground-colour is yellowish.
Subspecies and similar species	This species has both a wet-season form and a dry-season form: the latter is both smaller and more lightly marked. Similar is the bright yellow *H. leucippe,* and there are numerous subspecies of the above that are part yellow and form a transition between these two species.

107

♂

Scientific name	*Colotis regina*
Family	Pieridae
Common name	Queen Purple Tip
Wingspan	6 cm.
Range	South Africa, Rhodesia, Mozambique, Zambia Malawi, Tanzania, Kenya, Uganda.
Habits and habitat	Forest valleys and hills at lower elevations, savannah areas, and bush country. Flies all year round; generally local.
Food-plants	Probably Capparidae.
Sexual dimorphism	The female does not have the rich violet tip but instead two rows of small red-violet spots in the dark tip.
Subspecies and similar species	Variation occurs between summer and winter forms, as with all *Colotis*. Similar but less attractive are *C. ione* and *C. erone*.

108

♂

Scientific name	*Colotis danae*
Family	Pieridae
Common name	Crimson Tip
Wingspan	4·5 cm.
Range	Iran, Afghanistan, West Pakistan, India, Ceylon.
Habits and habitat	Found only in the hot lowlands, especially during dry periods. Always fly in the full, hot sun, often over rocky areas, briefly visiting flowers. Congregate around bushes of the food-plant, where they roost at night.
Food-plants	Cadaba indica, Capparis sepiaria, C. divaricata and Maerua arenaria.
Sexual dimorphism	The female is strongly dusted with grey around the body on to both wings; the tip is split and is duller in shade; across the hind wings there is a band of small grey spots.
Subspecies and similar species	The above without doubt came originally from South Africa (where there occurs the very similar *C. danae anna).* Considerable variation is found in the species illustrated, especially on the under side, between the dry-season and wet-season forms.